VIETNAM ADVENTURES
AND
RETIREMENT TRAVELS

Introduction

The stories are divided into fiction Vietnam Adventures, fiction Retirement Travels and nonfiction. The first two groups of nonfiction are absolutely as I remember them. The fiction stories are rambling thoughts that come from my demented mind.

© 2023 John H. Zimmerman Sr.

All rights reserved. No part of this book can be reproduced, stored in a retrieval system, or transmitted in any form by any means without the prior written permission of the publishers, except by a reviewer who may quote brief passages in a review or newspaper, magazine, or journal.

ISBN: ---------

Acknowledgments

Thanks to Karen, my beautiful wife of 60 years, whose encouragement and support were influential in my desire to write, a special thanks to my son, John Jr, my daughters Janet, Jennifer, and Janene for being there, and not forgetting Jackie and Kennedy our small dogs who would bark to wake me up when I fell asleep at the keyboard.

Dedication

I dedicate this book to all of my relatives who have served in the U.S. military:

Herbert Zimmerman (Father) US Navy WWII - Atlantic & Mediterranean

John William Zimmerman (Uncle) US Navy WWII - South America & Atlantic – KIA August 1942

Harold Stagg (Uncle) US Navy – WWII - Pacific -– Submarine

Ernie Lommatsch (Uncle) US Navy - Construction Battalion (CB'S) Pacific

Dick Diehl (Uncle) US Army—WWII - Europe

Gary Staggs (Uncle) US Navy

Jack Rozar (Cousin) US Army - Germany

Russell (Gene) Taylor (Son In-law) US Air Force - Desert Storm - Retired Colonel

Table of Contents

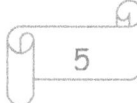

VIETNAM ADVENTURES	1
Introduction	2
Acknowledgments	4
Dedication	5
Table of Contents	5
Non-Fiction – Vietnam Adventures	8
Trip to Guam	9
Trip from Guam	13
Bangkok Adventure	14
Bien Hoa Deployment	15
Trip to Hue	18
Senior Chief John Wayne	19
Living in a Fishbowl	20
My 25th Birthday 1966	22
I Hate Snakes	24
The Consequences of Not Wanting to Shower with the Marines	26
Eating in Phu Bai, Viet Nam	29
Living in a French Villa	30
Deployment Odds & Ends	32
Returning from Viet Nam – 1967	33
Non-Fiction – Retirement TravelOur Travel Adventures	35
Travel update	49
November 2009 Jojoba Hills Temecula, California	55
Memorable Prose	56
Not Just Another Story	57
Checkpoint Able, Baker and Charlie	58
European Road Trip	61
The Spanish Motorcycle Cop	62
Visiting sites in East Germany	64
Paris Adventures	66
Trip to Desert Hot Springs	69
Vanhorn, Texas – Part 1	71
Vanhorn, Texas – Part 2	73

Van Horn & Texas I-10 – Revisited in 2010 75
Texarkana, Arkansas 79
Fiction – Retirement Travels 80
  Area 5X 82
  Uncontrolled Thoughts 84
  Just Another Day at the Office 85
  Observations 86
  Volunteering at Jojoba Hills 88
  Another Aggravation Met and Conquered 89
  Computer Things 91
  Unicorn 93
  Snakes on the Train 102
  Walking the (Alien) Dog 104
  The Origins of the Federal Amusement Park Marshals Service (FAPMS) 106
  Thoughts from Iowa 113
  Curse of the Lakota Chief 116
  The Sacred Cahuilla Tribal Stones 117
  The Briefcase Man 118

Non-Fiction - Vietnam Adventures

Trip to Guam

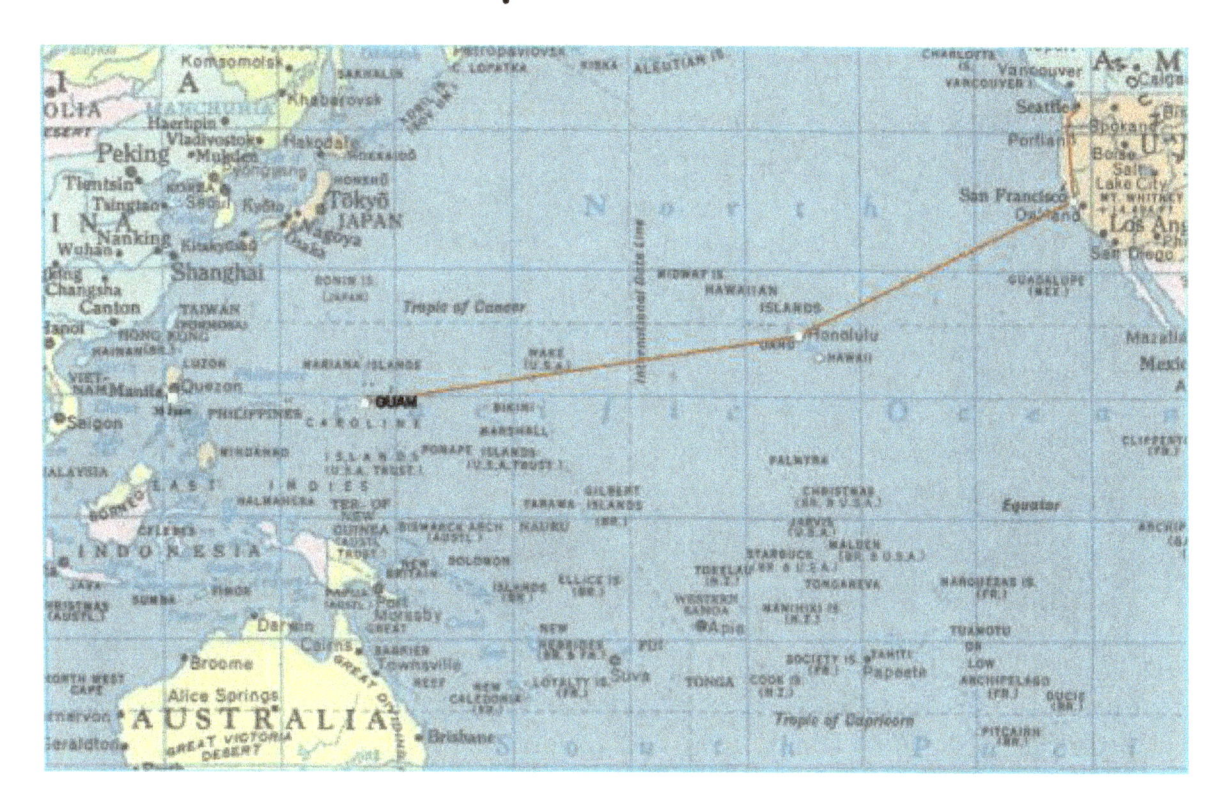

I took a bus from Los Angeles to Travis Air Force Base (AFB) outside of San Francisco. This was 1960 and I was 19 years old. In the excitement of going overseas to the exotic island of Guam, I forgot my dress blue cap on the bus and had to walk around uncovered until I could find my garrison cap in my luggage.

A flashback on my assignment to Guam is that about the time I got the assignment, a Japanese soldier from World War II was found on the island. From about 1944 until 1960 he had hidden in the jungle and did not believe the propaganda that the war was over, and that Japan had lot. He was finally captured and returned to Japan. Think of the promotions and back pay he was entitled to. All his military comrades were dead. Think of his wife, she thought he was dead and had remarried, his parents had died and what was there to go back to? The Japanese IRS probably met his plane to arrest him for not filing tax returns since he was not officially a POW during his stay on Guam.

At Travis AFB, I boarded a contract flight, meaning that it was a commercial flight with real stewardesses. It turned out that it was 24 hours flying time to Guam, with stops in Hawaii and

Wake Island. Speaking of Hawaii, the militarily refers to the United States as CONUS which translates into Continental Unites States. Hawaii and Alaska are offended by the OCONUS designation, which translates into (Outside of the Continental United States). There are 50 states in the United States and only 48 of them are in CONUS. This doesn't even consider the status of Guam, Puerto Rico, American Samoa, and the Virgin Islands which are US possessions.

This was 1960 in the days before jets; this flight was a four-engine propeller plane. Can you imagine flying for 24 hours and crossing the international date line?

After flying 24 hours we arrived in Guam the same day we left the United States.

Arriving on Guam in 1960, it felt like going back in time to World War II times. As I previously wrote, a few months before arriving in Guam a Japanese soldier who had been hiding in the jungle since 1944 was found and returned to Japan. While I was on the island a Japanese Zero fighter plane was found in the jungle only a short distance from the Governors Palace. I was stationed at the Air Force Transmitter site in Barragada. Our antenna field was full of bomb craters from American and Japanese bombs dropped in WWII.

The transmitter site was shaped like a cross with the top three sections making up the equipment wings. The bottom portion of the cross was two stories with the bottom floor containing the offices, equipment repair room, logistics, chow hall and a room that eventually contained a pool table. The top floor was the barracks, bathroom and day room which was furnished with a television and chairs.

Just after I arrived in Guam, we got a new OIC (Officer in Charge) and a new NCOIC (Non-Commissioned Officer in Charge). Under the old regime the logistics NCO (Non-Commissioned Officer) always ordered more supplies than we needed in anticipation of the day when he might not be able to get the needed supplies. He built up a 12 months' supply of most of the electronic parts that were required to maintain our communications equipment plus some that were required to sustain his after-hours TV repair business. The excess inventory was stored in the cable ducts under the floor in the transmitter equipment wing. These ducts were 4-6 feet deep and 4 feet wide and were full of excess inventory. When the new regime discovered the stash in the cable ducts, they pondered over what to do about the excess inventory. The process of ordering excess inventory was immediately stopped, and the excess inventory was to be returned to base logistics to be re-inserted back into the Air Force inventory, the only problem was that if the parts were returned to base logistics someone would have to explain where they came from and who was responsible for creating the excess inventory. Not wanting to get anyone in trouble it was decided to discard all the excess material in the deepest bomb hole in our antenna field.

I arrived on Guam at Naval Air Station (NAS) Agana. It was the only facility on Guam that allowed civilian aircraft to land. Anderson AFB was a SAC (Strategic Air Command) base and did not allow civilian access to its facilities. General Curtis Lemay was the commander of SAC, and he was a cigar chewing kick ass commander who had the final word on everything. In later years as Commander of the Air Force, he tried to convince President Kennedy to nuke Cuba during the Cuban Missile Crisis.

While on Guam I took two leaves, a five-day Rest and Recuperation (R&R) to Hong Kong and a seven-day leave to the Philippines.

Since Guam was considered a remote assignment, a five-day R&R was available to all Air Force personnel stationed in Guam. A C-54 would take you to Hong Kong and return you to Guam 5 days later. On the return trip several people had purchased bamboo furniture which filled up the whole plane. I purchased a suit and custom-made pair of shoes.
While in Hong Kong I had a "Catcher in the Rye" experience. I shared a room with a civilian who worked in the library in Guam. On the first night I was tired, and I went to bed early. During the night my new roommate came back and sat down on the bed and proceeded rub his hands on my chest trying to console me because I was in bed instead out seeing the town. He had returned to the room to pick up a jacket and as soon as he found it, he was out the door. I was uncomfortable with him rubbing my bare chest and feeling that I had been hit on, I immediately got dressed and I went out to see the town. For the remainder of the trip, I stayed out of the room as much as possible. I went up to see the boarder with China, ate on a houseboat restaurant where you picked out a fresh fish from and aquarium which they prepared for your meal, saw policemen directing traffic with a machine gun hanging over their shoulder, I saw

hundreds of house boats anchored so close together they made on big glob of boats, I took a cable car up to Victoria Peak, which offered a spectacular view of Hong Kong and the harbor.

The leave to the Philippines was not as structured. You went to the terminal at Anderson Air Force base and essentially hitchhiked a ride in a plane heading in your direction. I caught a hop on a C124 heading to Clark AB. Several people in my microwave training course at Keesler Air Force Base, Mississippi, were stationed at Clark, so I renewed old friendships and congratulated them on their good luck of not being stationed in Guam. I spent many hours in town visiting as many bars as I could while drinking San Miguel beer, which was ten cents a bottle. The black market was alive and thriving in Angeles, the town near the base. You could buy a carton of cigarettes on base for one dollar and spend the night drinking San Miguel beer plus have the company of a young lady for the night. I was 19 years old and had never experienced this lifestyle before. After seven days I was not ready to leave, so I sent a message to the first sergeant in my squadron on Guam requesting a three-day extension of my leave. After ten-days I caught a hop back to Subic Bay Navy Base, in the Philippines and then a short hop to Clark.

****

Trip from Guam

On returning from Guam in 1972 we again landed in Wake Island and Hawaii. On reaching Hawaii we were informed that the aircraft needed to have an engine changed and we would be put up at the Hawaiian Hilton until the plane was ready to continue to the States. We checked in and with a little encouragement from a Coast Guard seaman who had been stationed in Honolulu we headed for Hotel Street. Hotel Street turned out to be bar row or more aptly skid row. It was like bar row in any city in the United States. The bar was dark and smelled of stale whiskey, beer, and cigarette smoke. Since this was mid-morning, the only inhabitants were the locals who consisted of the biggest most intimidating Hawaiians I had ever seen. Since I was 19 years old, this was the first place where I could legally drink. After a few beers we headed back to the hotel. On reaching our room we were informed that the plane was ready to go, and we were to report to the airport immediately. We didn't even get to sleep in the hotel or gaze at the girls on the beach. What a waste of my first stay in Hawaii. The remainder of the trip was uneventful.

****

Bangkok Adventure

My first deployment from Clark Air Base (AB), in February 1966, was to Bangkok, Thailand in a C-123 aircraft pictured above. We loaded our equipment and truck and took our seats along the sides of the cargo bay on web seats. The pilot revved up the engines and headed down the runway and we were on our way to Bangkok, or so we thought. About one-hundred yards down the runway the pilot cut the engines and hit the brakes and we slowly turned around and headed for the hanger. A red warning light had started flashing on the control panel meaning something bad had happened so the pilot returned to investigate the problem. After a quick inspection it was found to be a false alarm and we again took our position on the runway and again headed off towards Bangkok, or so we thought. About 30 minutes out one of the radios went dead so once more we returned to Clark to have the radio repaired or replaced. After the repair was completed, we again took our position on the runway and again headed off for Bangkok, or so we thought. As soon as we were airborne the crew heard a strange thumping noise on the side of the aircraft, so once again or more accurately for the third time we returned to the hanger for a maintenance check. The aircraft is equipped with a static cable, to eliminate any static electricity, which is attached to a grounding point in the hanger during maintenance and is retracted back into the aircraft when maintenance is complete. Once the radio had been repaired on our last thwarted attempt to reach Bangkok, the maintenance man had disconnected the grounding cable from the grounding point but had neglected to retract the cable into the aircraft, so once we were airborne the cable was slapping against the side of the aircraft, thus the strange noise.

By now the passengers and maybe even the crew, were thinking it was time to try another aircraft. We had been on the aircraft for several hours, sped down the runway three times, been airborne twice and were still on the runway at Clark. We once again took our place on the runway, revved up the engines and sped down the runway. Finally, we were airborne and the remainder of the trip to Bangkok was uneventful.

****

Bien Hoa Deployment

At Clark AB we loaded our communications equipment and truck on a C-130 and headed off to Bien Hoa to install a microwave shot across the runway to provide communications for the Strategic Air Command (SAC) Detachment. We brought everything with us including two small canvas buildings, called Jamesway's, in which to house the communications equipment. The installation went flawlessly and within a week we had the communications link up and running. Over the next few weeks, we filled and stacked sandbags around the canvas equipment room on the main base to protect it from mortar attacks. The weather was so hot and humid that we could only fill two hundred sandbags each morning. We would then take a shower and head for the enlisted club where we enthusiastically proceeded to replace the bodily fluids, we had lost during the morning of filling sandbags. This went on until we had an eight-foot wall around the equipment room. In the four months I was at Bien Hoa we never came under attack, but the afternoons in the enlisted club were great.

Back in the early 50's Bien Hoa Air Base, Viet Nam was originally a French Air Force base. To help increase security the French laid mines around the far side of the runway, but when the U.S. Air Force took over the base in the early 60's, no map could be found of where the mines were buried. Strategic Air Command (SAC), the guys that flew the big B-52 bombers, sent a survey detachment to Viet Nam to survey the areas that would become radar sites for guiding aircraft on bombing runs. The survey and eventual operations groups was assigned to the 1st Combat Evaluation Group (1CEG). The idea was to direct the bombers to the target using ground radar and the digital maps created by the mapping detachment. They built their facility on the opposite side of the runway from the main base at Bien Hoa. They were not the only people on that side of the base; they had to drive through the U.S Army's 173rd Airborne camp to get to the SAC facility. The facility was about half the size of a football field and surrounded by a revetment which consisted of two 10-foot aluminum walls about four feet apart and the void was filled with sand. This kept the enemy out, but it pissed off the Airborne because they did not know why an Air Force detachment was in their base camp and why they needed so much security. One night, to work off their frustration, they threw several smoke grenades and flares over the wall into the center of the compound and retreated into the night. This caused mass chaos for the Air Force security guards until it was determined that they were being attacked by the Airborne. I'm sure that the detachment commander, a Colonel, called the Army Airborne brass to task over the nighttime attack...

On one of my trips over to the SAC detachment I picked up an Army Sergeant from the 173rd Airborne and gave him a ride to his compound. On my return trip he was walking back towards the main base, so I picked him up again. For giving him a ride, he invited me for a drink at the enlisted club. We joined eight other Airborne troops who had been there for some time. They had an upside-down fatigue cap full of money in the middle of the table. When the drinks came, they paid for it out of the hat. When the hat ran low everyone dropped in more money. I was the only leg (non-Airborne) and non-black at the table. We drank for several hours with everyone drinking the same thing, salty dogs (gin & grapefruit juice from a salt rimed glass). They talked about the battles they had been in and what they were going to do when they go out. The sergeant I had given a ride to the Air Force side of the base, tossed a Zippo lighter on the table. It was engraved with the battles that he had participated in and survived. That lighter would demand respect from anyone who understands what it signified. I think of that sergeant often and hope all his life's dreams came true from him, he more than earned them.

A few days later while making the trip to the SAC detachment I was stopped by the Air Force military police and given a ticket for having a dirty truck. I tried to explain that I would have to wash the truck every day because of the rain and the dirt road leading to the SAC detachment, but he was not impressed. I'm thinking the base commander wanted his base to look orderly and clean, so they cracked down on all the Air Force vehicles. The Air Force military police did not ticket any of the Airborne's vehicles.

Speaking of making a good impression, we had central showers which were about 30 yards from the barracks. On the trip to and from the showers you only carried a towel thrown over the shoulder and a bar of soap. Once they started landing civilian aircraft, which included female flight attendants, we were directed that we must be clothed while going to and from the showers. The war was becoming too civilized.

An NCO from the SAC detachment asked if I wanted to ride with him into Saigon to pick up some maps of the local area. Saigon was about 20 miles south of Bien Hoa. I pictured us being the only Americans on the road, but in reality, we were never more than ten yards away from another U.S. military vehicle. It was like driving in a twenty-mile convoy, military vehicles were everywhere. The trip was uneventful, but it leads into an adventure I was to have 6 months later driving into Hue.

About two months later six of the surveyors from the 1 CEG (Combat Evaluation Group), which was the unit for whom which we installed the microwave shot at Bien Hoa, were up in the Dong Ha area just a few miles South of the Demilitarized Zone (DMZ) surveying for a new radar site when they were all killed in an ambush. I heard that the Marines warned them that the area they were going into was not safe and they should have an escort, but they decided to venture out into the countryside without an escort. The war was becoming too uncivilized.

****

Trip to Hue

Just after I arrived in Phu Bai, Viet Nam I got a call from the Marine MPs in Hue saying that they had one of the airmen from our unit under arrest for drinking in an off-limits bar. They were going to hold him in jail until someone from our unit came to take custody of him. I asked where they were located and that I would be there in an hour. Hue was about ten kilometers north of Phu Bai. I would just follow highway 1 north for ten kilometers. I do not think there was highway 2, so I could not get lost. Highway 1 within Phu Bai was just like the highway between Bien Hoa and Saigon; it was filled with military vehicles. I grabbed my M-16, jumped in the truck, and headed north on highway 1. It took less than 3 kilometers for me to realize that highway 1 outside of Phu Bai was not the same as the highway between Bien Hoa and Saigon because I was the ONLY military vehicle on the road. The road was full of traffic, but they were all Vietnamese. I picked up a Marine hitchhiker in hopes that he would be going to Hue, but he was only going a few kilometers down the road. When the Marine got out, I put a round in the chamber of my M-16, engaged the safety and laid it in the seat beside me as I still had 7 kilometers to go...

I found the MP station, picked up the wayward airman, gave him my M-16 and headed back to Phu Bai. The rest of the trip was uneventful, with the exception of being scared as hell.

This adventure leads into my birthday adventure.

****

Senior Chief John Wayne

Let me set the stage for my John Wayne encounter I experienced in Viet Nam in late 1966.

He was a Navy Construction Battalion (Seabee) Master Chief Petty Officer and was a typical John Wayne character about 6'6" 280 pounds. Even though he was standing right in front of you he could be heard one hundred yards away, whereas I was an Air Force Staff Sergeant 6'2 150 pounds who listened attentively from a distance while the chief proceeded to chew out my men about stealing material from the CB's. They had acquired, I know not how, material to build a room in which we could put our refrigerator, attach a small room to eat in and construct a brick-and-mortar BBQ. Actually, it could be called a bar, party room and outdoor BBQ.

I walked up to Chief Wayne wearing only fatigue pants and shower clogs with no shirt and told him that I was the NCO in charge and if he had a problem with my men, he should have come to me and if necessary, I would chew them out. He did not appreciate my suggestion and now focused his rant on me. After a few minutes of venting his anger, he drove off in his truck and I never saw him again. I fanaticize that he knew that the scrawny Air Force sergeant was right and had the balls to stand up to him. In reality he probably decided that the situation wasn't worth raising his blood pressure over and he went back to the NCO club to replenish his bodily fluids.

****

Living in a Fishbowl

While at Phu Bai, Vietnam, we procured, and I did not ask how, some building material from the CB's and built a room in which we could keep our refrigerator, a counter to sit at, some stools to sit on and some extra room for a table and chairs, we called it "The Bar".

We did not have enough material for the walls, so we used clear plastic to keep the wind, rain, and sand out. Since at night it is dark outside, light inside and the sides were clear plastic, everything inside "The Bar" could be seen from 100 yards away.

One night everyone decided to go down to the Army MACV Compound about two miles up Highway 1. This is where the Army assisted in the training of new Vietnamese Army recruits. They had a real chow hall with tables with red and white checkered tablecloths and wine bottles with candles and Vietnamese waitresses. I decided that I would stay and watch our communications van while they all went to chow.

While sitting in "The Bar" engrossed in reading a book and possibly replenishing my bodily fluids, I was startled back into reality by several gunshots that could not have been more than 50 yards from "The Bar". It took me all of 5 seconds to realize that I was in a lighted room with clear plastic walls, and it was dark outside, and my every move could be seen from one-hundred yards away. I dove for the light switch and then fumbled for my M-16 which was hanging on the wall behind the bar. I chambered a round and waited for the next shots, which never came. I ventured outside to see what was going on. I saw two Marines yelling and waving their weapons in the air. They were about 50 yards away so I could not understand what they were yelling, but it couldn't be anything good.

Our communications van was surrounded by a 10-foot sandbag wall, and it was pitch black inside the enclosure, so I grabbed a flashlight and headed for the van. Once inside the sandbag enclosure I felt I could safely turn on the flashlight because it could not be seen from the outside. I walked around the van and kept the M-16 pointed where the flashlight beam was shining. I felt relieved that I did not find anything. The van was a mobile van which means that it was mounted on tires and was therefore about three feet off the ground. I decided that I should look under the van, just to make sure no one was there. As the flashlight beam and M-16 were sweeping under the van I was shocked to see two eyes staring back at me. My first thought was that it was a VC, and I should shoot him. Luckily for him I took a closer look, or maybe I was slow in pulling the trigger, and I saw that he looked like an American and he was wearing Marine fatigues. At this point I was no longer scared; I was pissed off. This SOB had almost caused me to shoot a Marine. I dragged him out from under the van and told him to walk towards the two shouting Marines or I would shoot his dumb ass.

It turned out that the two shouting Marines were MP's, and they were transporting a drunk marine to the local brig when he jumped out of the jeep and ran off into the night to hide under my van. They had fired several shots in the air to scare him, but only ended up scaring the hell out of me.

I only fired my M-16 once while I was in Viet Nam, but that's another story...

****

My 25th Birthday 1966

On my 25th birthday, July 30, 1966, I was in Phu Bai, Vietnam. Two of the airmen in our group had taken the truck to a bar about 5 kilometers north on highway 1. They were on a mission to purchase bar stools for the bar we eventually built with the lumber we had procured from the CB's. While they were in the Vietnamese bar discussing the purchase of the bar stool with the bar girls, two South Vietnamese Army soldiers, who were pissed off at the American soldiers fraternizing with their women, threw a hand grenade into the bar and another outside the front door, where our truck was parked. The grenade inside killed the woman setting on one airman's lap, which certainly saved his life, and the one outside destroyed our truck. The wounded airman was taken to the Marine hospital with shrapnel wounds. The medic said he almost died from shock, but that he was in good condition with only light shrapnel wounds. The hospital was really an aid station with litters sitting on two sawhorses. He was evacuated to Da Nang the next day and then to the Air Force Hospital at Clark AB in the Philippines.

Since our truck was out of commission with a destroyed gas tank, many holes in the body, and unknown engine problems the NCO in charge of our group, asked the Marines if they would send a wrecker to bring the truck back to Phu Bai. The Marines could not help us due to a lack of manpower but said we could barrow the wrecker and bring the damaged truck back ourselves. The sergeant accepted the offer and he with one airman and three Marines started the journey to get our truck. Getting there was not a problem, but by the time they got our truck hooked up behind the wrecker it was dark. The local Marine detachment told them that the road was not safe at night and suggested that they spend the night and return to Phu Bai in the morning. The sergeant didn't follow their suggestion and they started heading south down highway 1 towards home.

The sergeant was driving the wrecker with a Marine riding shotgun. One Marine was lying on the wrecker's bed with his M-14, and the remaining Marine and Airman were in the back seat of our truck which was being towed behind the wrecker.

A few miles down Highway 1 they were ambushed by the VC. The Marine in the wrecker bed started returning fire with his M-14 which immediately jammed. The Marine in the back seat of the towed vehicle had his 45 pistol in his hand which was hanging out the window and had pulled off 4 or 5 rounds before he realized what was happening. The airman in the towed vehicle started firing his M-16 out the back window, which had been blown out in the grenade attack at the bar. He went through one clip and had loaded a second clip when the M-16 jammed. He turned the rifle around and started kicking at the bolt to free the jam, but it never cleared. The Marine in the back seat with him thought the airman was going to shoot himself because of the way he was holding the M-16 and kicking at the bolt.

Someone was looking out for them that night. They made it back with no injuries, except for the wrecker. When they returned to wrecker to the Marines they counted over 40 bullet holes in the radiator, in the bumper, in the body right behind the drive and in the bed. There were no bullet holes in our truck. The damage pictured below was caused by the incident at the bar. Our unit in the Philippines sent us a new truck...

****

I Hate Snakes

We had two run-ins with snakes while in Phu Bai, Viet Nam.

The first encounter was in "The Bar". The Non-Commissioned Officer in Charge (NCOIC) was behind the bar and several Marines were on the other side on bar stools replenishing their bodily fluids with beer.

A word about "The Bar"; we brought our own generators to Viet Nam to power our communications van and to make life a little more bearable we brought a refrigerator to keep coke and beer cold. The Marines who were camped near us had no refrigerators and therefore no cold beer. In fact, Marines of the rank of E-6 and below could only get two beers a day and they were most likely warm. We bought the beer from the Marine PX for .10 cents a can, refrigerated it and resold it to the Marines for .25 cents a can. That, which we didn't sell, we drank or more accurately it was that which we didn't drink we sold…

Let's get back to the snake story. The sergeant behind the bar told the three Marines to climb up on top of the bar because there was a snake on the floor behind them. Of course, they thought he was kidding until they looked behind them and saw a poisonous green snake about a foot long on the floor. They immediately jumped up on the bar while the Sergeant looked for something with which to kill the snake. He ended up killing it with a chair, a club or maybe the butt end of an M-16, anyway that ended the first snake encounter.

The second encounter was several weeks later. I was sitting on my cot in our hooch when there was a commotion outside where we stored our extra junk.

A word about our hooch; when the site was set up our 10-man tent was erected on the sandy ground, and they used pallets for the floor. Since the tent supports were anchored in sand, one rainy windy night our tent blew down. We couldn't set it up in the wind, so we covered ourselves with the fallen tent and set it up the next morning. This is when the airman scrounged a tent platform from the CB's. The tent platform was a plywood floor on stilts about three feet off the ground and a shell over which we had to stretch our canvas tent. Now we had a real hooch off the ground which would not blow down in a rainstorm.

Oh yes, I was sitting on my cot in our hooch when I heard a commotion outside. I went our see what was going on and there was another poisonous green 18-inch snake outside our hooch, not 10 feet from my cot. The only thing I could think of was to shoot it, so I went in the hooch and grabbed my M-16 which always hung over my cot. I shot it and I know I hit it, but it just pissed it off, so I shot it again. Even hitting it twice didn't kill it, so someone got a shovel and cut its head off, which ended our second snake encounter. This was the only time I fired my M-16 while I was in Viet Nam. We thought that a Vietnamese had brought the snakes into our area in hopes that they would bite someone.

I almost forgot an important fact that affects the rest of the story. Between snake encounter one and snake encounter two, a Master sergeant replaced our original team leader. The first thing the Master Sergeant did was give everyone on site an Article 15 for not bringing their full tool complement to Viet Nam. After you lug an M-16, 200 rounds of ammunition, a 60-pound toolbox and a 60-pound duffle bag full of your clothes around several airports in Viet Nam, the next time you deploy you put the tools you will normally use in a small 15-pound bag and leave the rest at the base in the Philippines. The officer that came to Phu Bai to administer the Article 15's told us that once he got back to the Philippines, he would lose the paperwork, so we were not to worry about them ending up in our records.

Back to the rest of the snake story, on hearing my gunshots, the new Master Sergeant came out to see what was going on. On entering the hooch, he noticed the M-16's hanging over each cot. He asked if I kept a round in the chamber, I said that I did not keep a round in the chamber. He proceeded to inspect all the M-16 to insure they did not have a round loaded in the chamber. On the first two M-16 he removed the clip and pulled back the bolt, on seeing no shell ejected he released the bold reinserted the clip and returned the M-16's to their position above the cots. On the third M-16 he just pulled the trigger and sent a round through the airman's blanket, sheets, cot, and floor. It scared the shit out of him and since I saw that he had made a mistake by just pulling the trigger without clearing the weapon, he overlooked the fact that the airman had a round in the chamber and it was never discussed again. That was the first and only time that he fired an M-16 in Viet Nam.

****

The Consequences of Not Wanting to Shower with the Marines

The phrase "Marine shower" conjures up two images:

The first is that of a Marine getting back to the barracks after a day of training hard and sweating profusely. He is in a hurry to get to town to find a good bar and or a bad woman, whichever comes first, or both if he is really lucky. He strips down and applies excessive amounts of deodorant to various parts of his body, jumps into his civvies and heads to town.

The other image is that of a Marine base camp shower in Phu Bai, Vietnam in 1966 consisting of a shower tent with pipes running around the ceiling with small shower head every few feet to allow a spray of water to escape. The Marines stand naked under each opening and the water is turned on for 20 – 30 seconds, just enough time to get your hair and body wet. The water is then turned off for 20 – 30 seconds to allow the Marines time to wash their hair and other body parts, and then the water is again turned on for 20 – 30 seconds to allow time to rinse the soap and grime off. You are then done with your shower at least for the next few days...

I was part of a small Air Force unit providing communications for the 3rd Marine Division from Phu Bai to their headquarters in Da Nang. After experiencing the Marine shower several times, we decided that we would build our own shower. The shower can be seen in the background of the picture of a younger me. We had two 55-gallon drums welded together and laid them length wise on the roof of the shower. We connected a coiled garden hose from the drums to two shower heads and we were ready to take an almost private shower and we could use more than one minutes worth of water. The combination of the hot sun, the steel 55-gallon water drums and the coiled hose provided reasonably warm water for our showers. As for water, we had no running water at our site. The airmen attached to our team scrounged, and we didn't ask how, 30 five-gallon water cans. Every few days we had to drive to the water station and fill the water cans then lift them to the top of the shower and fill the two 55-gallon drums. We kept a little extra water in case we ran out before the next water run.

At the water station, the Marines added something to the water to keep it from killing you, but you had diarrhea for the first few weeks until you your body acclimated to the chemicals, just a little something to remind you where you were. To avoid the hazards of drinking water we drank beer or soda if no beer was available.

Our camp at Phu Bai was near the ocean which meant our tent and shower was built on sandy soil. To get rid of the water from the shower we decided to dig a three-foot-by-three-foot hole about four feet deep and let the water seep into the sand. This worked great for a few weeks but then the water just stayed in the hole. We made the hole bigger but that just made our small pond into a larger pond.

Since we had rats in the area the Navy medics would trap them to test them for plague. When one of the diesel mechanics doused a trapped rat with avionics fuel and set it on fire, the medics were not amused and told us NOT to set their rats on fire. When the medics noticed the pond created from the shower runoff, they told us that we had to get rid of the standing water due to the mosquito problem. We then decided that since we were on a small hill we would dig a trench from the hole, across a small dirt road and then fill in the hole and let the water run slowly down the hill. Again, this solution was great for a few weeks until erosion took over. Our small trench across the road turned into a deep gully which made the road impassable. Someone talked the CB's to into bringing a bulldozer over and fill in the gully and level out the road. This fixed the problem, but while filling in the gully, the bulldozer cut several Marine communications wires, and this was not good.

The Marines established highly successful Combined Action Platoons (CAP) which consisted of a rifle squad stationed in small villages to work with the local Popular Forces units to give the villagers medical services and security while disrupting VC and North Vietnamese Military activity in the area. Their main source of communication with headquarters was by landlines, which were the communications wires that the bulldozer cut while fixing our trench problem. The next day the Marines had to string new wires several miles to these remote villages.

The good news is that the weather turned cold. After a summer of temperatures in the high 90's with the humidity even higher, winter came dropping the temperatures to the low 60's. We were so cold that we had headquarters send us potbellied stoves to keep our tent warm. Due to the cold weather and the fact that the sun no longer heated the shower water, everyone stopped taking showers, which solved our erosion problem. We all started taking Marine showers as described in the first paragraph above, without much hope of finding a good bar or bad woman.

****

Eating in Phu Bai, Viet Nam

After eating in Air Force mess halls for 6 years I was accustomed to real china plates, real glasses, and real silver ware. At the end of the meal, we turned the dirty utensils over to someone else to wash. It was a shock the first time we ate with the Marines, they used metal trays with indented compartments, not China plates. We had to bring our own eating utensils and metal canteen cups. At the end of the meal, we had to scrape the remains of the meal into a garbage can, wash out trays, utensils, and canteen cup in a garbage can containing hot soapy water the rinse them in a third garbage can filled with hot rinse water. After enduring this for several days we decided to make other arrangements for our meals.

We scrounged C Rations from wherever we could and had the house girl bring in rice and French bread. The meals were not that bad; although I lost 20 pounds in the six months I was at Phu Bai. To break up the monotony of eating C rations we would eat with the regular Army unit down the road or even better we would eat with the Army MACV training unit. The MACV unit helped train the Vietnamese Army and they were living in an old French plantation house. They had converted the stables into individual rooms and for a few weeks, the team leader and I stayed in the stable rooms. It turned out that if you lived in the compound, you ate for free. Their mess hall had tables with red and white checkered tablecloths, candles on each table, and real plates, silverware, and glasses. They even had a menu and waitresses to take your order and bring your food to the table. Why eat with the Marines when the Army MACV is available?

I only remember eating one meal with the regular Army. It was duck and it was greasy and tasted bad, so I never ate there again.

****

Living in a French Villa

While stationed at Phu Bai, Vietnam in the last half of 1966, I slept on a cot. first in a 10-man tent pitched on the ground with pallets for a floor and later in 10-man hooch - a tent stretched over a plywood and 2x4 wooden frame with a plywood floor about three feet off of the ground. My cot was surrounded by a mosquito net, not only to keep the insects out but, as I was to learn later, to keep snakes out. To make the cot a little more bearable I bought a cot mattress that was stuffed with cotton, at least I hope it was cotton, from a roadside Vietnamese stand. You could buy anything from the Vietnamese roadside stands, included but not limited to almost any item sold in

I was an E5, Staff Sargant with an Air Force communications unit providing the Marines at Phu Bai with communications to their headquarters in Da Nang. Phu Bia was a little more rustic than we were accustomed to. We lived in tents, with a pallet floor, slept on cots, and we had to bring our own eating utensils and cup, which were part of our canteen and mess kit. The marines supplied a metal tray with several recessed compartments for different food items. When we finished eating, we had to wash the trays and utensils in soapy water and rinse them in clean water. This got old after a few meals.

We traded the CB's and Marines booze for C rations. The house girl would bring in French rolls and rice and we would combine them with C rations. On my payday trips to Da Nang to pick up our checks I would visit the class six store and buy several bottles of booze for trading for C rations. The reason I had to travel to Da Nang was that the paymaster out of the Philippines did not like traveling to Phu Bai, so I met him in Da Nang.

We tried eating with the regular Army on the day they had duck, and we vowed never to eat duck again. We stumbled across an Army MACV unit that assisted the Vietnamese with training new army recruits. They were headquartered about three kilometers north on highway 1 in an old French villa complete with a large dining room and horse stables, both of which become part of the story.

First the dining room. We started eating at the MACV Compound even though it cost two or three dollars a meal. The dining room had tables for four with red and white tablecloths, candles, real silverware and China plates, menus, a Vietnamese waitress that took your order and brought your food to the table, but best of all the food was great.

One or two nights a week they turned the dining room into a movie theater that showed TV shows that were popular in 1966. The ones that stand out in my mind were Combat and Gunsmoke, no touchy-feely chick flicks these. The rest of the week the dining room became the bar with a real bartender and waitresses.

When we deployed to Viet Nam, we brought generators to power our communications equipment and a refrigerator to chill our beer. We purchased warm beer and soft drinks from the Marine PX for 10 to 15 cents a can and resold cold beer and soft drinks to the Marines for 25 cents. The profit was used to throw going away parties or just "no reason" parties at the MACV bar.

During one of these parties, our NCOIC became friends with the Army MACV NCO's. He found out that he and I could move into a room within the compound and while we lived there all our meals were free, so we moved in the next day. The rooms turned out to be horse stalls in the stable area, which weren't that bad, but not what I expected my quarters would be living in a French Villa.

There were two rites of passage associated with newcomers living in the MACV compound. The first had to do with fresh water. The original French owners took advantage of living close to the South China Sea by using salt water for almost everything but drinking. This included the shower water in the stables. Now if you have never been in the Navy on a ship or have never taken a shower in salt water, you are not privy to one of the rites of passage – saltwater turns normal soap into a lumpy blob that will not rinse off, and you should never use normal soap as shampoo as it congeals in your hair and will not rinse out. What a mess, and nobody is going to forewarn you of your impending disaster. I was forced to walk back to our room with congealed soap in my hair and ask my roommate what the hell was going on with the soap. He just happened to have an unopened bar of saltwater soap that would solve my congealed soapy hair problem. One rite down and one to go.

No sooner had I gotten into bed when the alert sirens went off and we had to grab our M-16 and head for the nearest bunker. I did get my pants and boots, without sox, and grab my M-16 on the way to the bunker. This alert was for my benefit so I would know what to do in case of a real alert. Two down and I hoped that was all...

We only stayed in the stables for a few weeks, and we then moved back into our hooch, but we kept taking most of our meals at the French Villa...

****

Deployment Odds & Ends

When we deployed to Viet Nam, we were issued an M-16, 200 rounds of ammunition and 10 empty clips. The first thing we did was load the ammunition into the clips so that they were ready if needed. We were told to return the M-16 to the armory when we returned from Viet Nam, but that we did not have to return the Clips or Ammunition. This was a mistake. Over the period of six months, we accumulated over a thousand rounds of ammunition left behind by those returning to the Philippines.

One night two of the airmen loaded six hundred rounds of the excess ammunition and in a Marine jeep headed south down Highway 1 firing into the underbrush on both sides of the road. By the time they returned they had fired off all six hundred rounds. We had no reports of dead water buffalo or chickens, so I guess it was just an exercise in blowing off steam.

****

Returning from Viet Nam - 1967

In December 1966 I returned to the Philippines from Phu Bai, Viet Nam. I was on an eighteen-month tour in the Philippines but having spent ten months in Viet Nam my Philippine tour was reduced by five months. Having arrived at Clark Air Base in December of 1965, I was due to rotate back to the states in January of 1967.

On leaving Offutt Air Force Base, Nebraska in November 1965, heading for Clark Air Base, our plan was to bring Karen, John, and Janet to the Philippines as soon as I could get base approved housing. We also purchased a new 1965 Corvair which was to be shipped to the Philippines and was to be sold when we returned to the United States. As soon as I arrived at Clark AB, I put my name on the Housing list. Since there were a limited number of approved houses on and off base and I was in the middle of a big military buildup due to Viet Nam, we were in the three hundreds on the list. Ten months later my name finally reached the top of the list, but since I only had three months left on my tour, I turned down off-base housing.

After returning from Phu Bai in late December I was scheduled to return to the States in mid-January. Someone at squadron headquarters, thinking they were doing me a favor, scheduled me for a 5-day temporary duty (TDY) assignment to Hong Kong in mid-January. We had loaned the British Army some of our communications equipment and the squadron sent someone to Hong Kong every six months to make sure it was still working properly. The actual work would only take one or two days which gave you three or four days to enjoy the sights of Hong Kong. The only problem was that if I went to Hong Kong, I would have to delay my return to the US by several weeks, which I did not want to do. After being gone for fourteen months I was really looking forward to getting home. Needless to say, I turned down the trip to Hong Kong.

After landing at Travis Air Force Base, California, I went to Oakland Airport where I boarded a flight to Los Angles. I took the aisle seat in the first row of the aircraft because I wanted to be the first one off the plane. Only a few passengers got one plane in Oakland. We were off to Los Angeles, or so I thought, until only a few minutes into the flight they announced that we were starting our descent into the San Francisco Airport. The plane filled up at San Francisco. I thought it was a non-stop flight, but what would an extra forty-five minutes matter?

Then we were off to Los Angles, again. On approaching the Los Angeles Airport, it was announced that "Due to heavy fog at the Los Angeles Airport they were diverting to the Burbank Airport". Great, I would be the first one off the plane at Burbank with no one to meet me.
My parents were bringing Karen and the kids to pick me up at the Los Angeles Airport, not the Burbank Airport. It being the time before cell phones, I had no way to contact my family to let them know about the change in airports.

When we started deplaning at Burbank, I was made painfully aware that this plane had the exit stairs were at the middle rear of the aircraft, meaning I would be the last passenger off the airplane. As I descended the stairway, the terminal came into view, and to my amazement and relief there were Karen, the kids and my parents waiting for me at gate. It turned out that my mother had called the airport and was informed about the airport switch.

Even being the last one off the plane could not dampen my overwhelming joy of being reunited with my family.

****

Non-Fiction - Retirement Travel

Our Travel Adventures

In March 2007 we retired, sold the house, put our possessions in storage, bought a Ford 450 truck and a 36 foot Montana Big Sky 5th wheel and hit the road.

On our first trip out of Las Vegas was a loop from Las Vegas to the Black Hills then on to Yellowstone to meet the kids and lastly back to Las Vegas. Our first uneventful leg was to St. George, Utah, then on to Park City, Utah, and our $90.00 lunch (which included escargot, wine and some French cheese and salad).

412 Bistro – Park City, Utah

Our next stop was the KOA in Rawlins, Wyoming. For some reason we spent two nights there, then on to Gillette, Wyoming by way of Devil's Gate and Independence Rock both pictured below:

After spending several days in Gillette, Wyoming at the Crazy Woman RV Park (the only trailer park in town)

Our next stop was Sundance, Wyoming, and Devil's Tower...

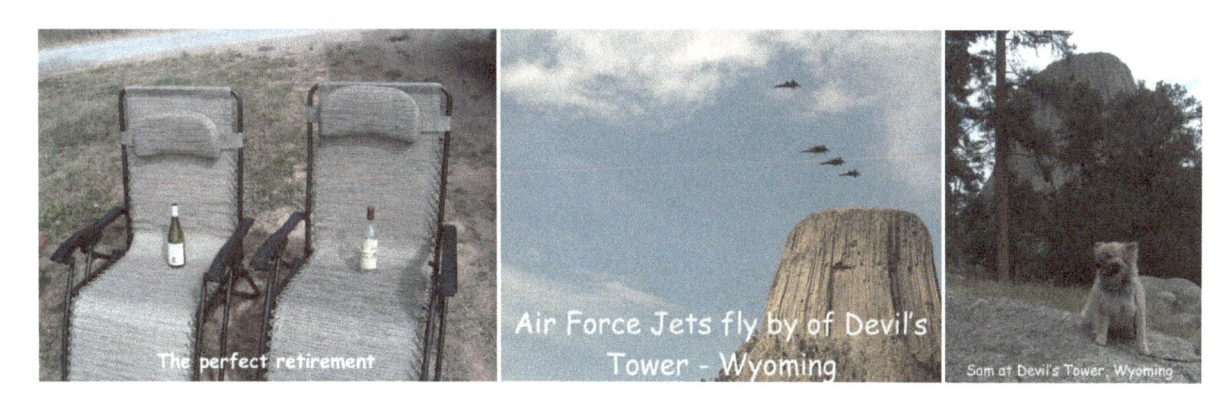

We then visited Deadwood, South Dakota, Sturgis, South Dakota the Black Hills National Cemetery.

Diamond Lil's Casino - Deadwood, South Dakota

Harley Dealership - Sturgis, South Dakota

Black Hills National Cemetery

We stayed at the Canyon Lake RV Park in Rapid City.

Karen & Sam at stream near RV Park at Canyon Lake Rapid City South Dakota

Karen's favorite store in Rapid City - Landstrom's Black Hills Gold

SOUTH DAKOTA AIR AND SPACE MUSEUM Ellsworth AFB - Rapid City, South Dakota

We then headed up to Hill City in the Black Hills...

On leaving Hill City, South Dakota, we went to Glendo, Wyoming to visit with Karen's cousins Terry and Lynn Bray. Terry and Lynn spend summers in Wyoming and winters in La Paz, Mexico.

Terry and Lynn Bray's Yard decorations in Glendo, Wyoming

Terry and Lynn Bray's Yard decorations in Glendo, Wyoming

Our next stop was Thermopolis, Wyoming. We went on a Dinosaur dig and soaked in the hot springs…

Karen at Dinosaur dig site near Thermopolism Wyoming - 2007

Fossil bed near Thermopolis, Wyoming

Teepee Fountian - Thermopolis, Wyoming

Next, we were on to meet the kids at the Goff Creek Lodge, just outside the east gate of Yellowstone. The only problem was that there were fires at the east end of Yellowstone, and they closed the East gate and they all had to exit out the north gate and circle around through Custer, Wyoming, and the back towards the East Gate. This detour added about 100 miles to their trip. The kids got cabins and we parked the 5th wheel in the front yard with electricity and water.

Goff Creek Lodge -Out East Gate of Yellowstone Park, Wyoming

The next day we all went into the park to see Old Faithful and the mud pots at the main lodge. Lennon got sick and I took him back to the Lodge. As we were heading for the East Gate, we noticed the fire was in the hill close to the East Gate Exit. About 15 minutes after Lennon and I went through the gate, they closed it due to the proximity of the fire. This meant that once again the kids had to exit by the North Gate and drive one hundred miles through Cook City and Custer to get back to the lodge. We did not venture into Yellowstone again…

Cabins at Goff Creek Lodge - Near Yelowstone, Wyoming

Cook City, Montana

While in Flagstaff, Arizona we drove out to see Meteor Creator.

Meteor Creater, Arizona

Karen at Meteor Creater, Arizona

Meteor Creater, Arizona

Nellis Air Force Base –

The first picture is the Flag inside Thunderbird hanger at Nellis AFB. The second picture shows flags of countries in which the Thunderbirds had performed. And the last picture is of first female Thunderbird team member, Captain Nichole Malachowski.

Crossing Bolder Dam and the construction of the new bridge to bypass the dam...

Kevin Costner playing at the Surf Ballroom in Clear Lake Iowa, which was the last place that Buddy Holly performed before being killed in a plane crash in a corn field just a few miles away.

September 2009   **Iowa State Fair, Des Moines, Iowa**

I have never seen so many food vendors; I now understand why so many people are overweight…

September 2009   **Museum – Kearney, Nebraska**

October 2009   **Cliff Dwelling Museum - Colorado Springs,**

November 2009 - The Reagan Library in Simi Vally, California

November 2009   **Pismo Beach – Arroyo Grande, California**

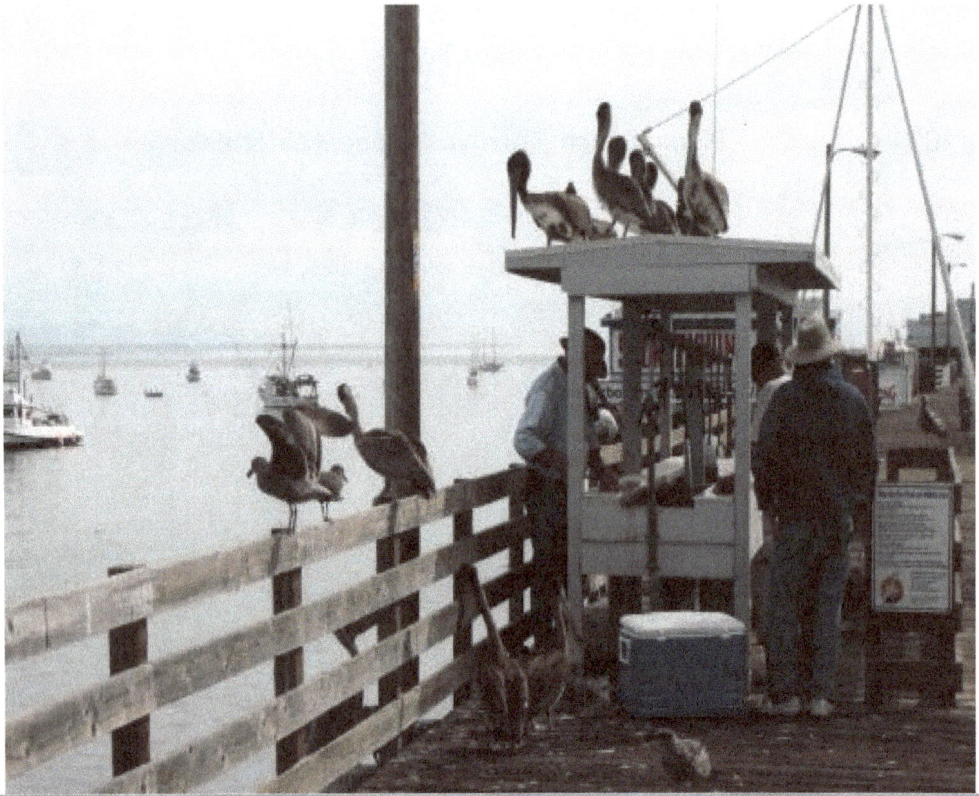

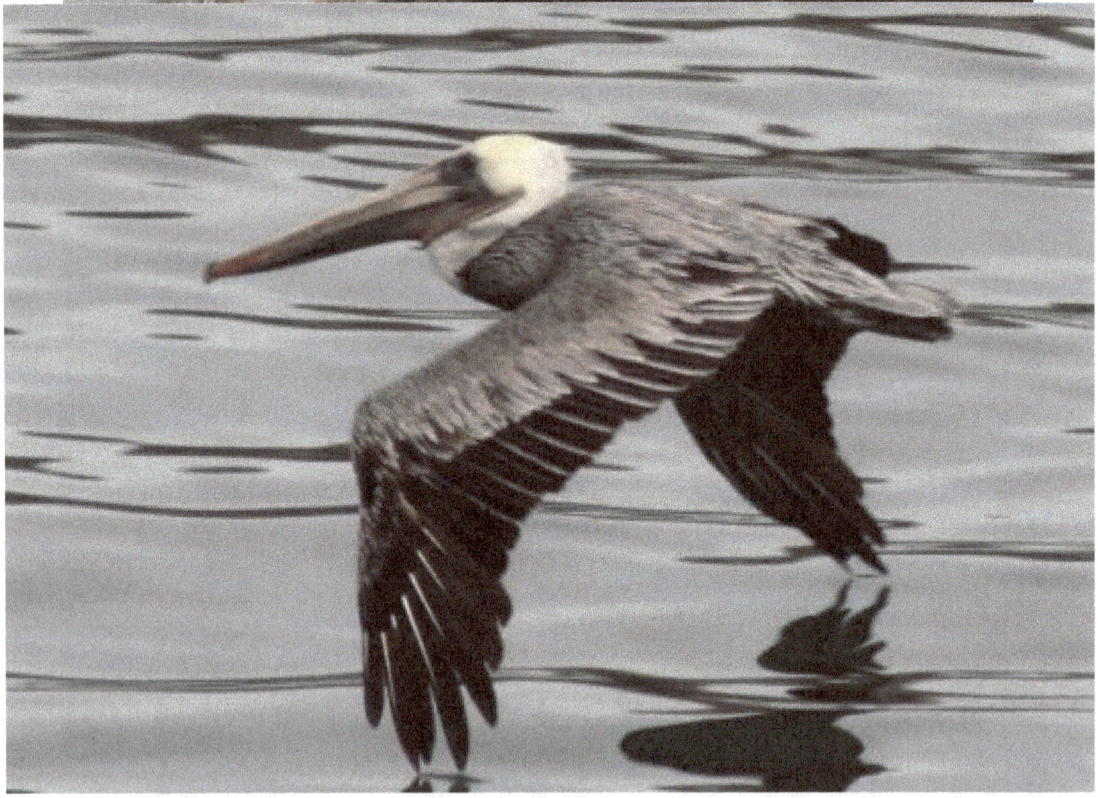

Travel update

October 2, 2010
We made it to Branson, Mo yesterday.
We spent three days at the Lost Lake RV Park near Hermann, Mo.
Hermann is a major stop on the Missouri wine trail.
We only visited three wineries, but that was enough...
First let me say that I hate backing the RV into an RV space, and I really hate it when there are trees, and the road is narrow.

While attempting to back in, you cannot give me instructions on which way I should be turning, you can only tell me when I am about to hit something.
All of the above were factors in my repeated attempts to park at the Lost Lake rv park and during this time I repeat all of the four-letter words I have learned in the last 69 years...

After about thirty minutes it was close enough and we set it up for our three day stay.

Oh yes, one thing we forgot when leaving Iowa was to lay our wine cabinet down so that the bottles were standing upright.

During the first hard right turn I made, the wine cabinet tipped over, luckily none of the bottles broke, but I had to crawl over the island cabinets and clean up the mess before I could pop the slides out.

We are staying at the Treasure Lake RV Resort in Branson. Whoever designed this park had never been in an RV in their life. The roads are too narrow, the electric and water hook ups are too far from the RV and the topper is that the sewer connection is on the opposite side of the RV, which places it right outside your front door, that is if your sewer hose reaches that far...

After making Karen endure two of my parking tantrums, I agreed to take her to any show she wanted to see in Branson.
Let me first say that I dislike musicals and shows with animals...
You guessed it; we are going to see Noah, a musical about Noah's ark, with real live animals. She is getting payback for my RV backing tantrums...

Our next stop is Oklahoma.

See you then...John and woman who is taking me to a musical...

October 6, 2010
We are now in Thackerville, Oklahoma. Thackerville is only three miles north of the Red River, which is the border between Oklahoma and Texas.

October 8, 2010

We arrived in Canton, Texas today. Canton's claim to fame is the "First Monday Trade Days", which is advertised as the oldest and largest Swap meet in the world. The population swells from 3,300 to 300,000 at the height of the summer swap meet season. Thanks to the swap meet, the RV Park we are staying in is booked every weekend through April 2011. The only other redeeming factor is that Bonnie and Clyde stayed at the Dixie hotel, which we could not locate as it may have been torn down.

October 11, 2010

Today was not the best of days.

Since we left Iowa thirteen days ago, we have had great weather. Every day was sunny with not a cloud to be seen. This morning started with overcast skies with intermittent mists of rain warning you that it was going to pour down soon. The second indication that this was not going to be just another pleasant day in Texas came from the GPS. Its initial indication was that our travels this day would be 275.9 miles. The problem with this calculation is that it is the line-of-sight distance, not actual road miles. Once the GO button was depressed it updated the mileage to 345.5 miles, which makes for a six- or seven-hour driving day. Several hours later we reached Interstate 35, which is the North/South Road between Dallas and San Antonio. Since we were headed from the Dallas area to the San Antonio area, I deduced that we would be heading South on I-35. When we were ready to enter I-35, the GPS lady told me to turn left onto I-35 NORTH. The direction was correct, but the GPS was screwing with my mind with the NORTH. I double check the words on the screen, and they indicated the same thing the GPS lady said, they were both screwing with me. I turned left and headed South on I-35 and the GPS approved my decision. Just outside of Bandera, Texas we entered a two-lane road. The first bad sign we saw read "NO passing for the next 78 miles", meaning it was a narrow curvy road for the next 78 miles, but luckily, or as it turned out unluckily, we were only going about ten miles. The next un-nerving sign read "County maintenance ends here": my first thought was then who was filling the potholes? The next dilemma that developed was a sign reading "Curve to the left – slow to 30 mph". Thinking that this meant that the main road curved to the left, I followed the direction on the sign and slowed to 30 and drove to the left. The GPS immediately went into "recalculation" mode, meaning that I had taken a wrong turn. The GPS lady started telling me to turn right at these little dirt roads, and I could see myself having to back out of a dead-end dirt road, and you know how much I hate to back up with the 5th wheel. Finally, we came to a dirt road that was wide enough to pull a u-turn; the only thing I did not notice was the low hanging tree branches in the path of my u-turn. After making the u-turn Karen noticed a door handle in the road and thinking it was of our RV I jumped out and retrieved it.

The good news was that it did not come off our RV, but that was the extent of the good news. The low tree branches had torn the roof fabric in several places and had also broken one of the plastic vent covers. I will spend the next few hours patching the damage. To top off our day, it turns out that the PV Park we are spending two days at should have been rated a one or two star, not a four star.

October 12
In surveying the damage to the top of the RV, it is a little more extensive than two or three fabric tears. There are 12-18 tears in the roof fabric, the ladder is demolished, two plastic vent covers will need to be replaced, the gutters on each side need work plus the plastic light cover was trashed. Oh yes, the door handle that Karen saw in the road turned out to be part of the ladder, so there was NO good news...

These repairs, the black tank problem, the water leak behind the shower and a few other odds and ends should keep the RV in the shop for a few weeks...

We have adjusted our itinerary as follows...

Deming, New Mexico – Oct 14 – 16th.
Apache Junction, AZ – Oct 16 – 18th.
Thompson RV Service, Colton, Ca - Oct 18th until???
Monday night Football – Oct 18th...After our latest Texas adventure, we are in dire need of a Monday night football party...

We decided to venture into Bandera to get diesel, see what town was like and eat a late lunch. I had my heart set on Bar-B-Q ribs and there was only one such restaurant in town. After strolling around the two blocks of downtown Bandera we headed for the rib joint only to encounter a sign saying they were closed on Tuesdays, and yes this was Tuesday. We only have two days left in Texas. If I ever give the slightest indication that I am driving through Texas again, please just shoot me...

October 13, 2010
We are now in Ft. Stockton, Texas. The good news is that today was a good day, and the better news is that tomorrow will be our last day in Texas

October 14, 2010
At last, we are out of Texas. We are spending two days in Deming, New Mexico

October 18, 2010
We finally arrived in California and dropped the RV off for repairs. It turns out that the roof damage will be between 7 – 9 thousand dollars, but the insurance will cover most of it. So much for a "little" roof damage. They are estimating that the repairs will take 2 – 3 weeks.

October 20, 2010
Today we arrived in Las Vegas. We will spend a week or two here while the RV is being fixed. We left Iowa September 28th and have had great weather for the next three weeks until we came to Las Vegas. When we arrived at Janene's it was raining so hard that we could not get out of the truck for about 10 minutes.

October 22, 2010
I was awakened out of a deep restful sleep, well that's not quite true. Most sixty-nine-year-old men have not had a deep restful sleep in fifteen years. Between getting up every few hours to visit the bathroom and not being able to get back to sleep because you are reliving your life in detail, you tend to require a nap every afternoon. But I regress. At 5:30 this morning a knock at the door and four barking dogs woke everyone. It was the Las Vegas Metro Police. They asked me to check my truck to see if anything was missing. I am usually meticulous in making sure the truck is locked, but I must have experienced a senior moment. Of course, I found that the GPS was missing. Having to go through life with no GPS means I would have to rely on Karen to read the map and convey timely accurate directions, which has not worked very well in the past. The GPS was a marriage saver. But again, I regress. The police had found my GPS in the thief's backpack several blocks away. Let me regress again, with cigarettes costing $50-$60 a carton, Karen has taken to rolling her own. She buys loose tobacco and cigarette tubes and with the help of a tube stuffing machine she rolls her own cigarettes saving $25 – $30 a carton. Getting back to the police story, the thief had also taken two cartons of empty cigarette tubes, which I told the police belonged to Karen because she rolled her own cigarettes. I was prepared to recite the story of why she rolled her own, but he didn't ask so I didn't tell. The thief must have been in a hurry or scared or both because he took the $200 GPS and completely missed the $500 camera not a foot away. It is now apparent why the thief has a chronic unemployment problem; he does not pay attention to detail…

Until next time...

John (the GPS reliant driver) & Karen (the non-map reading navigator)

November 7, 2010
The latest status on the RV is that it SHOULD be ready by Friday, November 12th.

The insurance on the RV will cover 5 days of hotel and meals, so today we are checking into a hotel casino in downtown Las Vegas. We have not stayed downtown in 15 – 20 years.

When I had the oil changed before leaving Iowa, they found that the differential had a leak. I decided to wait until we got to Las Vegas to have it fixed. I took it in for repairs on October 27th. They did not complete the repairs until November 3rd, first due to a lack of mechanics as one was in a training class and second due to a lack of the correct tool, which they had to order. Luckily, the extended warranty covered the cost of a rental car for the duration of the repair. Now we just need the RV, and we will be on the road again.

November 20, 2010
The latest status on the RV is that it SHOULD be ready on the afternoon of November 23rd. When they were drilling a hole to install the black tank they mistakenly drilled into the black tank. They are having another black tank shipped by air and it is to arrive on Monday and installing it immediately. We will drive down from Las Vegas on Monday, stay in a hotel, and pick the RV up on Tuesday afternoon. It has taken over a month to complete all the repairs. So much for the two-week estimate.

November 24, 2010
We arrived at 11:00 a.m. to pick up the RV, and low and behold all the repairs were completed and it was ready to go, well almost...

They had forgotten to wash the road grime from the RV. This only took 20 minutes but saved me $60.00 because I didn't have to get someone to wash it.

Now comes the bad news. We have been full timers for almost 4 years and in that time, I have hooked up the RV to the truck several hundred times. The process is easy but repetitive. You get the RV latch mechanism at the right height to be accepted into the truck latch mechanism, you open the locking bar on the truck receptacle and back the truck up until the RV mechanism latches into the truck mechanism and the locking mechanism closes, thus locking the RV to the truck. Having done this several hundred times, I skipped the final step, which is to visually verify that the locking bar is in the locked position. You can probably visualize what transpired next... As I slowly pulled the truck forward, the RV came off of the truck locking mechanism and landed on the sides of the truck bed causing a small amount of damage to the sides of the bed, but luckily no damage to the RV. Remounting the RV to the truck, as previously described, is normally an easy operation except that when "shit happens" it happens in multiple instances.

When the landing gear is raised too high it blows the fuse, which of course is the first iteration of "shit happens". The landing gear fuse is in the battery compartment in the front of the RV. I retrieved the box of fused from inside the RV and placed the open box on the rear bumper of the truck. To access the battery compartment, you must be on your hands and knees because it is located under the front overhang of the RV. When I tried to open the battery access door, the twist latch rusted and would not open. Now I had to dig out a wrench to get the twist latch open. After opening the compartment and replacing the fuse the only thing left to do was to stand up. In using the truck bumper as a support to assist in standing up of course I spilled the box of fuses, so here I was on my hands and knees picking up the scattered fuses. After uttering several four-letter words beginning with D and S and another letter close to D. I proceeded to get the RV re-mounted on the truck and the rest of the day was uneventful.

One final note: The complete bill for this visit to RV doctor was a little over $12,000, $10,000 of which was the tree damage...

****

November 2009 Jojoba Hills Temecula, California

Memorable Prose

In an old, and I mean really old, Humphrey Bogart "B" movie.
He meets a woman on a cruise ship. When a friend asks him to describe her, he says, "Do you remember the girl you almost married in high school". Nothing else need be said because this simple statement conjures up not only memories but feeling of that long ago high school sweetheart.

From "Berlin Game" by Len Deighton:
"Did you ever say hello to a girl you'd almost married long ago? Did she smile the same captivating smile, and give your arm a hug in a gesture you'd almost forgotten? Did the wrinkles as she smiled make you wonder what marvelous times you'd missed? That's how I felt about Berlin every time I went back there."

Alexis Carrel
"Searches for light in the darkness of the world."

Officer and a Gentleman (David Keith's Sid Worley character says when he first sees Lisa Eilbacher's character)
Bodacious Tata's

Nelson Demille - "Up Country"
"Whoever controls the present controls the past."
In reference to present day Vietnamese interpretation of the battle of Khe Sanh.

Originally from Orwell's 1984:
"Whoever controls the past controls the future and whoever controls the present controls the past."

Edmond Burke
"All that is necessary for the triumph of evil is that good men do nothing."

****

Not Just Another Story

This story began in November 2009. I was having trouble with tires on the RV as is evidenced by several previous horror stories. I had the shackles replaced with the version that can be lubricated every few thousand miles. If you are wondering what shackles are, so am I. They connect to the axels and wheels and seem to keep everything in alignment; I hope that makes sense, if not read the damn story anyway…

Why the RV manufacturer used cheap shackles is obvious, they were trying to save money and make a greater profit at my expense. Anyway, I was told to lubricate these fitting every few thousand miles, so in December 2009 while I was at Wal-Mart, I purchased a roll around dolly that I could lay on and roll around under the RV and a manual grease gun so I could lubricate the shackles when I was rolling around under the RV.

I carried the roll around dolly and grease gun in the pickup for nine months and today, September 20, 2010, was the day. We are leaving Iowa in one week, and it was not raining so I thought it was a good time to lubricate the shackles.

I broke out the dolly and assembled it, put the grease gun together and proceeded to roll under the RV. The first problem was that I am almost 70 and getting down was an extremely slow process, like in slow motion play back you see on TV on Monday night football. Once there I tried to roll under the RV. The first problem was that the ground was asphalt and really old asphalt which was extensively pitted, which impeded my ability to easily roll around. It took several minutes to maneuver the six feet to the axel area when I discovered the second problem, my stomach would not fit under the axel, either the RV sits really low, or I need to lose some weight. I must be the low thing… I finally got in position to see the shackles but now the third problem became evident, I could not locate the grease fittings on the end of the shackles. I was just about to call the RV shop that installed the shackles and find out what the hell they did with the grease fittings when I felt on the side neatest the tire, which I couldn't see, and guess what; the grease fittings are on the side nearest the tire which means that the only way to lubricate the shackles is to jack up the RV and remove the tires. Why would they install the grease fitting so that you had to remove the tires to grease the shackles, it is obvious; they want you to bring it back to them so they can charge you to grease the fittings. Since they must remove all four tires, they can now charge you (me) $100.00 to grease four fittings.

Now I have a dolly and grease gun for which I have no use. Tomorrow, I will donate them to Good Will.

****

Checkpoint Able, Baker and Charlie

In late 1989 we took a driving trip to Berlin. We drove from Frankfurt am Main, opposed to Frankfurt (Oder) which is in the former East Germany. Prior to driving to Berlin, each person traveling had to apply for special military orders which were written in English, German and Russian. These orders allowed you to enter the Russian sector of East Germany at Checkpoint Alpha and exit the Russian sector into the American sector of Berlin at Checkpoint Baker.

When Jennifer, Janene, Karen, and I arrived at check point Alpha I took the orders and passports into the Russian checkpoint while the women waited in the van. The Russians had what looked like an old bank teller's window, except they had replaced the window with a piece of plywood so you could not see who was on the other side or what they were doing. I slid the passports and orders through a hole in the plywood and waited for what seemed like 10 minutes until they had finished whatever they were doing and slid them back to me with just a curt "OK".

When I got back to the van, I noticed what looked like a 16-year-old Russian Army guard wearing a long wool overcoat and carrying a rifle slung over his shoulder walking around the van. I found out later that the girls had been making faces at him. The only visible uniform was his overcoat and boots and given the pathetic state of the Russian Army stationed in East Germany, we wondered if that the only thing that he was wearing.

At the briefing I received when I picked up the orders back in Frankfurt, I was told that if anything happened in the Russian sector that I was not to speak to the East German guards but was to only speak to the Russians. It seems that the East German guards were not friendly with Americans. The drive through East Germany to checkpoint Baker was uneventful.

When we attempted to enter East Berlin through Checkpoint Charlie the US Army sentry suggested that we go back to the hotel and leave anything that identified us being attached to the US military and bring only our passports. So, we left our military ID cards, ration cards, military driver's license and any other things that would indicate we were not just ordinary tourists. We entered East Berlin using only our passports, again slipping them into a hole in the plywood window and waiting while did whatever they did. When the passports were eventually returned that contained a sheet of paper which turned out to be our visa to enter East Berlin.

Jennifer, Janene & Karen
At the Wall - Berlin, Germany - 1989

East German Patrol Boat in Berlin.
They offered Jennifer & Janene a tour of the river.

While in East Berlin we visited the Pergamon Museum containing the Ishtar Gate, which was one of the interior gates of Babylon dating from 575 B.C. by King Nebuchadnezzar_II.

The Germans completed construction of the gate in 1930 using material excavated from Babylon.

While walking in West Berlin along the Spree River that separated East and West Berlin, an East German Patrol boat pulled up to the shore near where we were walking. They were not being extraordinarily vigilant in their duties of patrolling the river; they had maneuvered their patrol boat towards our side of the river so they could talk to Jennifer and Janene. They spoke enough English to offer the girls a tour of the river. Karen and I were about twenty yards from the river's edge and the patrol boat; whereas the girls with only about five yards from the patrol boat. I could picture an international incident in the making and hoped the girls had enough sense not to get in the boat. This cold war confrontation continued for about fifteen minutes before the East Germans decided it was time to get back on patrol.

On leaving Berlin I again slipped the orders and passports through the opening. After several minutes, a note emerged through the hole asking if I wanted to buy any Russian Army patches. The thought flashed through my mind that if I said no, I may never see our passports or orders again. After thinking about it for two more seconds I said, "No thanks", after what seemed like an eternity the orders and passports miraculously appeared in the opening with another curt "OK". I gratefully grabbed the papers and jumped in the car and took off for Checkpoint Able. Checkpoint Able, on reentering Germany is manned by the US Army. When I told him them about being offered Russian Patches by the Russians, they asked if I had purchased anything from them, I said "No" with which he replied, "Good, because if you had purchased anything I would have to confiscate it and arrest me, because US military personnel were not allowed to purchase anything from the Russians." I told him to get screwed because I was not a US Military Personnel and jumped in the car and headed for Frankfurt.

****

European Road Trip

We were racing north on the autobahn near Munich, Germany trying to reach Amsterdam before it got dark. The distance between these two cities is 510 miles. In the US this trip would take about 10 hours, but we made it in a little over six hours. We even stopped for gas and a bite to eat. You do the math. We were cruising at between 100 and 110 miles an hour most of the way and didn't even get a speeding ticket, but we were frequently passed by Mercedes and Porsches.

Let me regress somewhat. When we arrived in Germany, we purchased a new 1989 Dodge Caravan. We chose the caravan to accommodate a wife and two teenage daughters. If you have ever had the exhilarating experience of traveling with a wife and two teenage daughters and their baggage, and by baggage I refer to suitcases (if emotional baggage were to be considered I would have purchased two cars - mine and theirs), you know why the Caravan was selected. On one trip to move our youngest daughter from England to Germany, we removed the third seat, and the back was filled from floor to ceiling with all her worldly belongings. Not wanting to delve into the mess in the back of the van, when we came through customs in Belgium, they just waved us through.

****

The Spanish Motorcycle Cop

While living in Germany we took a vacation to Spain. Lisa, a friend and co-worker of Karen's, and Lisa's mother joined us, and we stayed in a villa, and I use that word loosely, which belonged to another of Karen's co-workers at the Rod & Gun club at Rhine-Main AB, Germany. The word villa invokes a vision of elegance and opulence which was lacking in our villa, but it was clean, fully furnished, and free. We were about 20 miles from the Mediterranean. We drove down to the beach several times and I remember sitting in a sidewalk café drinking coffee, it was very European.

We drove into Barcelona and looked around the city, had lunch which I'm sure included a few beers. On the drive back to our villa the beers induced an inhuman urge to answer nature's call immediately. I saw a gas station on my left about 100 years ahead, which seemed too far, but it was the only choice in sight. I set my mind of turning left into the gas station and relieving myself very soon. As I approached the entrance to the gas station on the left, I turned on my left turn signal and proceeded to slow down in anticipation of relieving myself very very very soon. At the point I noticed a Spanish motorcycle cop on my side of the road motion me to continue forward and NOT to make a left into the gas station and therefore not to relieve myself anytime in the near future. It only took about two seconds for me to decide that this was not the course of action that my body wanted me to follow, so I made the turn and drove as close to the entrance to the bathroom as I could get, not noticing that the Spanish motorcycle cop was right on my tail. As I jumped out of the van, the Spanish motorcycle cop was there waiting for me. In my haste to relieve myself the only thing I could say was, "Please excuse me I MUST go to the bathroom." , and with that I rushed past the Spanish motorcycle cop and headed to the bathroom. When I came out, he was still waiting for me.

He was the coolest Spanish motorcycle cop I had ever seen, not that I had seen that many, but he was cool. He was slim, trim, and young and had a two-day growth of beard. He was wearing black leather from head to foot, with black shiny boots that came up to his knees.

In perfect English he asked me if I had seen him motion to me not to make the left turn. I said that I did see him, but nature was really calling loud, and I had no choice but to make the left turn. He said turning into the gas station on this busy highway had caused many accidents. He was there to make sure no one turned left into the gas station. I apologized profusely many times and told him I would not do it again. I also apologized for not talking with him when I jumped out of the van, but I had no choice.

During this time the three women were in the van thinking this was really funny. Here I had drunk a few beers which caused me to make an illegal left turn and brush past the Spanish motorcycle cop in my rush to relieve myself, and now I was trying to explain why I had ignored the Spanish motorcycle cop's instruction NOT to turn left.

After about what seemed like an hour of him telling me what I had done wrong and apologizing profusely he let me go with a warning to drive carefully.

Now the only problem was that to continue on our journey home I would have to make a left turn out of the gas station and cross the busy oncoming traffic. Using my better judgment, I decided to make a right turn and find a place to make a u-turn.
The rest of the trip was uneventful.

****

Visiting sites in East Germany

In 1992, we visited the ruins of the Church of Our Lady in Dresden which was destroyed in the bombing of Dresden on February 13, 1945. The Russians, who occupied East Germany from 1945 until 1989, would not allow the cleanup of the rubble created when the church was destroyed. They wanted it to remain as a reminder of the destruction the Americans unleashed on the Germans. Some of the stones had recently started to be collected and cataloged, but most remained where they had fallen in 1945.

The church was rebuilt and reopened in 2005.

****

Paris Adventures

While living in England we visited Germany several times. On one trip we took a side trip to visit an engineer living on the Mediterranean in Cannes, France. In Germany restaurant food was not a problem because German food was basic food, not the exotic unknown foods of France. While visiting France the only thing Jennifer and Janene would eat was French Onion Soup, because they know what was in the soup. At one stop I ordered a sausage meal to show the girls that the food was good and ok to eat. The sausage had such a foul order that I could not eat it, so I ordered French onion soup.

On reaching Cannes our friends talked us into staying in the summer cottage at the house they were renting. I may have forgotten to mention that we visited Cannes in December. We accepted their hospitality, not knowing that winter nights in Cannes get extremely cold and that the summer cottage did not have central heat.

They provided us with a small portable electric heater that kept blowing the circuit breaker in the house. Our friend would reset the breaker, but when it tripped after they went to bed, we had to wait until the next morning for heat.

An example of how cold it gets is that the pool had a log floating in it and when I asked why, I was told it was to keep the ice from forming in the pool. In fact, they used the pool to keep their wine chilled.

We endured the circuit breaker problem for two nights and then moved into a hotel in Cannes. The rest of the stay was great. We drove over into Italy, came back thru Monte Carlo, and visited the shops and beaches of Cannes. Karen and the girls visited a perfume factory and purchased several bottles of perfume, which almost got us in trouble with British Customers.

A word on the beaches, they are topless beaches which conjure up various vivid images of beautiful French women sunbathing topless. But as I previously mentioned this was December and the only topless woman on the beach was a 70-year-old woman who should not have been topless, so much for my images of the topless beaches of the French Rivera.

Our stop in Paris was uneventful and we caught the ferry back to Dover, England. On clearing British Customs, the agent asked if I understood the items and quantities of items that could be imported into England. I told him that yes, I thought understood the rules. Being an American I thought he would just wave us through, and we would be on our way, but he asked me to open the trunk and asked me to open one of the travel bags. Luckily, it was not the one with the bottles of perfume. He only wanted to see the one bag and told me to continue through the check point. If he had found the perfume, it would either have been confiscated or we would have had to pay a large import duty and possibly a fine. Occasionally someone watches out for dumb Americans.

On another trip to Paris, Jennifer had the map, and I was negotiated the freeway into Paris when the freeway went into a tunnel and started winding under Paris. It turns out that years later this is the underground freeway in which Princess Diana was killed. We picked an exit and ascended from the underground maze and miraculously ended up one block for our hotel. When I pulled up in front of the hotel the sign said we could park there over the weekend, this being Friday afternoon we ended up parking twenty feet from the front door of the hotel. We were staying just across the Seine River from Notre Dame and just blocks from the restaurants in the Latin Quarter.

The rooms were on the third and fourth floors and the elevator was 100 years old and would only hold two people at a time. If you walked up you would beat the elevator. We loaded the suite cases on the elevator and let it carry them up to our floors. The rooms had recently been remodeled even though the elevator had not. The ceiling was covered with a sheet of white plastic stretched tight a few inches below the real ceiling, but you could not tell how they attached it to the wall.

We ate good food, visited the Louvre, Eiffel Tower, and Arc De Triumph, walked the Champs-Elysees, and ate more good food. We all climbed to the top of the Arc De Triumph. Jennifer, Janene, and I climbed to the first level of the Eiffel Tower while Karen waited for us on the ground. What is the name of the restaurant in one of the legs of the Eiffel tower?

On leaving Paris when I turned on the heater fan, I heard a grinding noise, and a puff of dust came out of the heater vent. When we got back to Harrogate, I took the heater fan apart and found the remains of a mouse in the fan cage. I could have been fined for importing an animal into England without going through the quarantine process. Rabies does not exist in England and all animals entering the country must be quarantined for six months to ensure they do not carry the disease.

****

Trip to Desert Hot Springs

We arrived at Desert Hot Springs, Ca. late yesterday and will be here for two weeks. This turned out to be another one of our recent exciting trips that I could have done without.

We were ascending a steep grade about 15 miles southwest of Needles, Ca. when the engine started overheating. We only had four pints of drinking water, so I added them to the radiator. Since we were on a narrow two-lane road, I had to ascend the mountain for another few miles before I could find a place to turn around. I kept worrying that it would start overheating before I could find a place turn around. Luckily returning to Needles was all downhill so it did not overheat again.

It took almost all of two gallons of anti-freeze (at $20 a gallon) and two gallons of distilled water to fill the radiator.

I just added "Check Radiator Level" to my pre-flight checklist. No more radiators overheated during the rest of the trip.

On leaving Blythe, CA I had 1/4 of a tank of fuel and I didn't even think of filling up because I could go at least 80 miles on that amount of fuel. It turned out that the next gas station was 86 miles down the road. When we pulled up to the pump the computer in the truck indicated that we had enough fuel left to go ONE more mile, which probably equates to 6 cups of fuel...

I'm glad that someone is looking after the idiots in this world...

Then to top it off, it turns out that the RV Park is less than a mile from the San Andreas Fault, which is the most active fault in the North America. Now I can add worrying about the BIG ONE to my list of experiences I can do without.

January 15, 2010, update:
Today we found ourselves again on US 95, the highway between Needles and Blyth. My only thought was that I had not checked the radiator level before leaving Laughlin that morning. My worrying was for naught as we had an uneventful trip. Well not quite uneventful. We were headed for the Black Rock RV Village on highway 60 in Arizona. The address on the reservation confirmation e-mail was in Salome, Arizona, so I entered Sloan in my GPS, and we were off to see the wizard. On reaching highway 60 the GPS lady told me to turn right, and the Black Rock RV Park would be half a mile on the right. When I reached the point the GPS lady had

indicated, I was in the middle of the Arizona desert with nothing visible for miles in any direction, except more desert. I continued a little further and finally found a sign showing Salome was about 10 miles in the opposite direction. On reaching Salome we could not find the Black Rock RV Park, or the address indicated on the e-mail. I tried calling them on my cell phone only to find that my phone didn't work. Luckily, Karen's phone was working, and I contacted the RV Park I was told that the address on the e-mail was their mailing address and RV Park was located on US 60 about 25 miles west of Salome in a town called Brenda, which is not in my GPS or on any map we had.

Except for having gone about 40 miles out of the way, the rest of the trip was uneventful.

****

Vanhorn, Texas - Part 1

Have I got a story for you…?

It started in late 1960. I was in the Air Force and had just graduated from electronics school in Biloxi, Mississippi. I was given 30 days leave before departing for an 18-month assignment on Guam. I had my car in Biloxi and to save money I had two buddies chip in for gas in exchange for a ride to California. My car was a bitchen 54' two tone grey two door Oldsmobile 88. Our route was from Biloxi, Houston, El Paso, Phoenix and then into California ending in La Puente.

For some unknown reason we picked up a hitchhiker in Louisiana or Texas and he said California sounded great. Then for some completely unknown reason I let him drive. I had no idea if he knew how to drive or even had a driver's license. Because he talked about a sister in Fort Worth, we kept an eye on him to make sure he didn't start heading north towards Fort Worth.

I almost forgot, because I wanted drive as much as possible, I was popping "No Doze" to stay awake. They were in all probability pure caffeine, and they did keep me awake, but not from hallucinating. At one point while driving on Interstate 10 in Texas, I slammed on the breaks because I saw a car's headlights heading directly for us. After the car passed us about 50 feet to the left, I noticed we were on a divided highway and decided to let someone else drive.

The bitchen car broke down in Van Horn, Texas. The mechanic did not have the part but found one at the Oldsmobile dealer in El Paso - 120 miles west. Since this was in the days before credit cards, you could not ask them to ship it and you would pay them later. The only thing I could do was hitchhike into El Paso pay for the part and bring it back. One of my Air Force buddy's and I tried for about 30 minutes to hitchhike wearing civilian clothes, but no one would stop. We decided to change into our uniforms.

My buddy was the nervous type and said whatever came into his meager mind. The first car that came by stopped and the wife rolled down the window and asked what happened. Before thinking my buddy said," The fucken car broke down and we need to get to El Paso to get a part." The wife immediately rolled up the window and told her husband to step on it…

Needless to say, I told my ex-buddy not to talk until he got to his house in California. The next car that stopped took us all the way to the Oldsmobile dealer in El Paso and we decided to take the bus back to Van Horn. This adventure only cost us a 24-hour delay.

The remainder of the trip was uneventful with the exception of having a blowout just outside of Blythe, California. I have already told you my Blythe story. We changed the tire and cruised on into La Puente with no further problems.

This sets the stage for the rest of the story…

On leaving Las Cruces, NM this morning, I had to make a u-turn on a divided highway. I cut the turn too sharp and the left RV tires rolled up over the divider curb. At the next light I got out and check the tires and all looked well. About 170 miles later I thought I saw something fly off the tire on the left, but the tire looked good in the side view mirror. I was only 5 miles from, you guessed it, Van Horn, Texas, so I decided to stop for fuel and check the tires. Since I was now in Van Horn, Texas I really didn't have to look at the tire, but I did anyway. A 6-inch by 3-inch chuck was missing from the side wall of the front left RV tire and it was slowly going flat. This adventure only cost us about a 2-hour delay…

On our trip back to Las Vegas we will be taking Interstate 40 because it doesn't come anywhere near Van Horn, Texas, and I will make no more upturns on divided highways…

****

Vanhorn, Texas – Part 2

Now here is the rest of the Van Horn, Texas story...Here we go again...

This will be my Johnson City/Austin story.

Johnson City has only a few stores a gas station and a Post Office, but it is famous because it was the home of President & Ladybird Johnson. It is now also infamous because it is the location of our second blowout in Texas in two days. The left rear tire, of the legendary "u-turn on a divided highway" incident, blew about 10 miles out of town. We drove for another few miles to Fridays General Store and Gas Station. I called our Emergency Road Service provider for the second time in two days and waited for two hours to get the tire changed. At 5:04 PM I called the RV Park in Austin and left a message that we would not arrive until about 8 PM, but everyone must have gone home because no one answered my call. We arrived at the RV Park at 8:30 to find the office closed, but an envelope with the name Ocerman was in the late arrival box. I figured they had misspelled my name, so we parked in the space indicated for Ocerman. At 8 am the next morning the park manager knocked on the door and said we were parked in Ocerman's spot, and they had no vacancies. I told her that over the past two weeks I had left several phone messages, sent an on-line registration, and finally talked to a woman who indicated our reservation was ok. It finally got straightened out and they found a place for Ocerman.

Our next challenge was when I decided to replace all of the tires on the 5th wheel with Michelin tires. I called Costco and they had the tires in stock but first needed to know the torque pressure required for the lug nuts. After several phone calls I found I had the answer in the RV owners' manual. Next, they wanted me to bring the 5th wheel in today to make sure they had to equipment to change the tires tomorrow. Let me regress a little here. I have not become proficient in backing up the 5th wheel; in fact, I suck at back up the 5th wheel. The RV spot we got in Austin was a back-in with trees on both sides. It took me 30 minutes to get it in with a lot of help from a friendly neighbor. For me to intentionally leave the site and have to back in again was absolutely out of the question. I would rather listen to ex (thank god) President Bush talk about WMD's than back into an RV spot. I called Discount Tire and had the tires changed the next morning.

We were on the road to Texarkana by 11 am...

I am now seriously considering taking I-80 back to Las Vegas mainly because it does not come anywhere near Texas...

I will be writing a Texarkana story soon...

****

Van Horn & Texas I-10 – Revisited in 2010

Last year I vowed to never again drive on I-10 through Texas. This is because I had two blow outs on the 5th wheel last year and one the year before. This year because I want to keep to the southern route and miss the really cold weather, I-10 is the only option. Therefore, in preparation for our plunge into the unknown adventures awaiting us on our 2010 Van Horn & Texas I-10 travels, I took a vow of celibacy to ensure my mental and physical energies would be peaked. Of course, at sixty-eight, peaked does not conjure up the same images it did forty years ago. Back then peaked was analogous to the spiraling heights of the Rocky Mountains, today it could be compared to the rounded mounds of the sand dunes at Pismo Beach.

Though I do not take the vow lightly, I did not want to prolong the period of chastity, so I waited until the day prior to entering Texas before initiating the vow.

To demonstrate my newly acquired energy, we tempted fate by entering Van Horn, Texas to refuel. We even stopped at the same station at which I discovered our tire problem last year; it may have even been the same pump. Not wanting to tempt fate more than necessary we did not linger in Van Horn, we refueled and got out of town. My energy prevailed and the stop in Van Horn was without incident.

Our next test will be Johnson City, Texas. If we can make it through Johnson City, my newly acquired powers will be validated.

As proof of the potency of my new energy, the above picture is of Karen by the Lyndon B. Johnson National Historic Park in Johnson City, Texas. Below is the Silver Circle K Cafe.

We spent several hours in Johnson City and ate at the Silver Circle K Cafe, which is housed in the old lumber yard. Not wanting to overstay our welcome and use up too much of my newly acquired energy we delayed the touring of the LBJ Ranch and Western White House until another time. By then I may be brave enough to try the visit without taking the vow.

Before we could get out of Austin my strength must have waned because the evil Texas snow god descended on Austin, and we had a snow day...

The demented Texas snow god demonstrated her power was greater than mine by loaded the top of the 5th wheel with two inches of snow. When I tried to pull in the slide outs, the snow blocked them from fully retracting, which forced me to climb up on the roof and remove the built-up snow from the top of the slides. To make matters worse, sometime in the past I had backed into an object and broken the bottom two rungs of the ladder attached to the back of the 5th wheel. To overcome this, I had purchased a beautiful ladder which folded up nicely and fit in the bed of the pickup. The only problem was that I left it in Las Vegas in Janene's garage. My only option was to use a stool to bypass the bottom two rungs. Much to my amazement I climbed up the ladder, swept off the snow and made it down the ladder without falling off the roof. My energies prevailed; the vow paid off…

The last test is to traverse the 20 mile stretch of I-10 that exits Texas and enters Louisiana which we will attempt early next week. This stretch of highway is undoubtedly the worst I have encountered in my travels across the United States. Two years ago, we had a blowout on the 5th wheel on this part of I-10.

In the past two years the stretch of I10 described above had been repaired and most of the road was in good condition, with the exception of the bridges. The roadbed had been repaved, but the bridge surfaces were extremely uneven and caused the 5th wheel to bounce unmercifully.

The good news is that the vow worked and the trip out of Texas and through Louisiana was without incident.

The bad news is that Karen is now going to use the success of the vow to reinstate the vow every time we venture out onto the road, even if it's just a trip to Wal-Mart…

Sometimes you just can't win…

****

Texarkana, Arkansas

The description in the RV Park book for Texarkana is "Lots of shade trees and a good place for walking or just sit under a tree and rest." On arriving at the RV Park, in no way would I describe it as a good place for walking or sitting under a tree. Even when it was new back in the 60's it was not a nice place to walk and relax, it was across the street from a railroad switching year with trains running all night and blowing their whistles just to annoy you. The concrete pads on which you are to park your RV, and all cracked and broken, the small brick walls that once supported a flower garden were all falling apart, the grounds had that wild unkempt look and the park manager left at 5 PM and did not return until 10 AM. This doesn't sound like the description in the RV Guide. Since the office did not open until 10 AM, the procedure for paying for the overnight stay is to place $15 in the envelope provided and drop it in the slot at the office. As luck would have it, we only had $20 bills, so we ended up paying them $5 extra for staying in their mediocre park.

Several days later I was looking through the RV Guide and noticed that the above description of trees and a restful setting was describing the park in Texarkana, Texas; we stayed at the park in Texarkana, Arkansas.

****

Fiction – Retirement Travels

Area 5X

In 2009 on leaving Colorado Springs heading for Las Vegas, I made a startling discovery. In *retrospect* it was purely by chance that I uncovered the location of Area 5X. Area 51 is a well-known non-existent government installation and if there is one such non-existent installation, there are undoubtedly many more...

Traveling west on I-70 from Denver, we encountered snow about 10 miles before entering the Eisenhower Tunnel. It was snowing heavily when we entered the tunnel but sunny and clear when we popped out of the other end. Pushing it a little past our normal 300 miles a day, we arrived at the local RV Park in Green River, Utah just as the sun was setting. One of the cardinal rules of RVing is not to pull into an RV park after dark. Parking and setting up in the dark can be a real pain.

Let me give you a little background on Green River, Utah. Green River is 360 miles west of Denver on Interstate 70, and 180 miles southeast of Salt Lake City on Interstate 15 and State Route 6. In 1961 the government built a missile launch complex between Moab and Green River to test fire missiles towards White Sands Missile Range 400 miles to the south. The official word is that it was abandoned in the early 1970's.

I woke up about 3 am and could not get back to sleep, so I did what every rv'er would do, I went to Wal-Mart. Traffic in Green River is non-existent at 3 am. On entering the Wal-Mart parking lot, the only other vehicle I saw was the Wal-Mart resupply semi pulling into the receiving bay. The strange thing about this particular truck was the low-profile auto tracking satellite dish mounted on top of the trailer. Why would they need a television satellite receiver on the trailer that delivers inventory to the stores?

On entering the store, I had a strangest feeling that something was not quite right, but I could not figure out what it was. Although I get a strange feeling every time, I enter a Wal-Mart because every one of them is configured a little bit different, sometimes the food is on the left and the pharmacy on the right or during construction they turned the plans over and everything is opposite. Pet supplies can be anywhere, and they take great pleasure in stocking the RV supplies in a different place in every store. But the feeling I had this time was different. It wasn't until I was checking out that it came to me, all the employees were under forty years old, with most in their early twenties. Then I remembered that when I parked my truck the parking lot was empty. Where did the employees park their cars? So, I went back to the RV to think about what I had just seen, or not seen.

The next day, after lunch, I took my wife back to Wal-Mart to show her what I had seen. First the parking lot was now half full, and the employees were back to normal, meaning most of them were in their sixties and were most were working to supplement their social security. I asked the checkout clerk what time the late shift started, and she said midnight. On the way out I checked the delivery truck parked at the receiving bay and it did not have a satellite receiver on the roof. Of course, my wife thought I was crazy, but that is her normal opinion of my state of mind, but just maybe I was living up to her expectations…

At eleven thirty that evening I drove down to Wal-Mart to watch the delivery truck arrive. I didn't have long to wait as the truck was already backing into the receiving bay as I was walking around to the back of the store. As I watched the unloading of the truck, I was perplexed by the sight of them not unloading boxes of merchandise, but of unloading people. Between twenty and thirty people exited the delivery trailer and entered the store. My first thought was that they were smuggling illegals to work in the store, but most of the people getting off the truck were white, and I could not detect an accent with the exception of maybe Southern or Bostonian….

In trying to figure out how they had dug a tunnel from the Wal-Mart to the secret base especially how they had disposed of all that dirt, it finally hit me that they did not dig the tunnel from the store to the site, they dug the tunnel from the site to the store.

****

Uncontrolled Thoughts

The bad news from Iowa is that the temperature has been in the 90's with the humidity in the same range.

The good news from Iowa is that due to the extremely hot temperatures the women dress appropriately or inappropriately depending on your outlook.

I have come to the conclusion that I may not revive my beard.
I have invested too much time and money in sculpturing my facial features over the years. It has taken almost 68 years of living, 46 years of marriage, a lot of good wine, more good beer, some great scotch, tons of good food, some bad women, a few good woman, four children and six grandchildren to create the facial features I display to the world, why hide all that effort behind a beard?

****

Just Another Day at the Office

It all started back in March of 2007 in Las Vegas, Nevada. My partner and I, who coincidently is my wife, were on assignment with a government agency that will remain unnamed. I was assigned to a team investigating possible attempts to infiltrate a classified installation near Las Vegas. Since Russians were not allowed to travel in Nevada, they were attempting to recruit agents with blackmail through gambling and prostitution. I volunteered to test the Russians blackmail attempts, but much to my dismay my partner would only let me test to gambling hypothesis.

This is the first paragraph of the beginning of a story of which I have no idea where it is going…

****

Observations

Jim prided himself being extremely observant of what was going on around him and being able to absorb this information and deducing what was not obvious to the normal person. The only problem was that his deductions were not always in line with reality, like the time when he was 14.

Jim was going to the local mom and pop grocery store to pick up something that he thought he really needed. He noticed that the florescent sign and the outside lights were out, and it was only **8:45 pm** and the store didn't close for another fifteen minutes. This was not normal. Jim entered the store, but no one was in the store. He knew that when Mr. Nash, the owner, went to the stock room, he would flip a switch under the counter by the cash register that made a buzzer ring when the front door opened. The buzzer did not go off when Jim opened the door, so Mr. Nash had forgotten to flip the switch, which again was not normal.

Jim then noticed that the key was still in the cash register, which would allow anyone to open it and take what they wanted. Mr. Nash always took the register key with him when he went to the stockroom. Something was very wrong. He then saw something that confirmed his suspicion; a woman's purse was on the counter by the cash register. What woman would leave her purse alone in a public place while she left the room? It had to be ROBBER. The gunman had taken Mr. Nash and the woman into the stockroom to tie them up or maybe worse.

Jim moved quickly to the curtain that separated the stockroom from the main store. He could hear something, but it was muffled and sounded far away. He slipped through the curtain and walked slowly down the hall. He could hear a little better now. The robber must have been getting ready to do something bad because he could just make out the woman saying "Oh God no! Oh God no!" Jim slowly peeked around the corner and saw that on top of the boxes of baby food and women's private products the robber was getting ready to forcefully seduce the woman.

Jim jerked back into the hall and tried to think of what to do. He knew the robber could not chase him because his pants were down around his ankles, but he didn't want the robber to recognize him, so he got a pair of panty hose off the shelf and pulled them over his head. He then got a cup of scalding hot coffee from Mr. Nash's ever brewing coffee pot and threw it at the robbers bobbing butt. As the liquid was sailing through the air, seemingly in slow motion, Jim noticed the robber was not forcefully seducing the woman, Mr. Nash was. No, Mr. Nash was not forcefully seducing the woman either, because she was not pleading "Oh God no!" she was moaning "Oh Todd go!" Mr. Nash's first name was Todd. As the hot liquid hit Mr. Nash's bobbing buttocks his muscles contracted in surprise and the woman moaned, "Yes!" When the burning sensations reached Mr. Nash's brain, he jumped up slapping his buttocks with both hands and yelled things that should not be said in front of a woman or a 14-year-old boy.

In the brief second before Jim panicked and ran, he recognized that the woman was Mrs. Simmons the Head Librarian. Jim was out the door and down the street within three. He ripped the panty hose off his head and ran straight home without stopping. Jim never went into the store again and he only went to the library when was sure Mrs. Simmons was not working. He heard that Mr. Nash had to take a few weeks off, because on a burn on his back side; while he was mopping up, the mop handle broke the coffee urn behind him, and the coffee spilled on him burning his back side. That's when Jim learned that passion and fear bring out similar actions and reactions in people and that in the future he must closely examine and then re-examine his conclusions before acting.

****

Volunteering at Jojoba Hills

Volunteering is the mainstay of Jojoba Hills; it is how the RV Park was built 20+ years ago and how it is maintained today. When we arrived, I decided that I would follow the tradition and find a position that I would volunteer for and perform it to the best of my ability.

As I perused the list of available tasks, I found one that instantly perked my interest; it was simply listed as *Street Walker*. Those two words conjured up vivid imagery. I envisioned a lamp post on a dark street. I was smoking a long slender cigarette, smoke curling up around my head, hat pulled low over my eyes with my back against the post. I was watching the procession of ladies of the evening leisurely sauntering past my lamp post...

After letting my imagination run rampant for several more minutes of the vivid sauntering imagery, I asked what the duties of a Street Walker entailed. Much to my dismay I was informed that the Street Walker was responsible for keeping the streets and roadways of Jojoba Hills clear of debris which consisted mainly of errant pebbles from gravel driveways.

I thought what the hell and volunteered to become the Street Walker of Jojoba Hills. In my youth I loved to kick rocks on the way home from school. I was soon to learn that as I had progressed in years my agility had diminished somewhat; you notice how deftly I avoided the "getting older" phrase. In earlier years I could spot a pebble the size of a pea at ten yards and adjust my stride to approach the object much like a skillful football kicker and place myself in perfect position to punt the errant pebble expertly off the road. Lately the pebble has to be the size of a walnut and I am usually half a step off and somewhat off balance and, more often than not, my foot completely misses the errant object. I have learned to recover gracefully thus concealing my diminished agility. In my youth I was also skillful in angling an object to the right or left to return the pebble to its original locale. I can still compute the required angle much like a professional pool player, but due to the reason stated above, I completely miss the pebble.

So if you see me walking the streets and back alleys of Jojoba Hills with my head down, I am not depressed, I am searching for errant objects. If you see me stumble and almost fall, I most likely have not been drinking, you are just viewing my failed attempt to boot the errant object off the roadway.

****

Another Aggravation Met and Conquered

Being a full time Rv'er, my main aggravation must be backing the 5th wheel into a tight camp site. Aggravation may be too weak a description of my feelings towards backing the 5th wheel (dislike intensely, loath, hate, detest) one of these would be a more appropriate description. Running a close second to my intense dislike of backing the 5th wheel is setting up the satellite dish. After a few traumatic episodes of attempting to set up the dish for short stays in RV parks, to keep my sanity I decided not to set up the dish unless we were staying a month or longer.

The problems centers on mechanically adjusting the elevation and skew on the dish and then point the dish to the correct azimuth. Even though the elevation and skew have adjustment scales they are small, and my eyesight is not what it was fifty years ago, or even ten years ago. Once those two mechanical settings are made, the last problem is pointing the dish in the correct direction. To accomplish this, I bought a small Boy Scout compass which should get me close, but never seems to. On three separate occasions after house of attempting to set up the dish, I have become so frustrated that I called the local cable guy to come and set up the dish for me. To further emasculate me it only took the cable guy twenty minutes to completely set up the dish and the receiver and collect fifty dollars from me.

We decided to treat ourselves nice and bought a pre-Christmas present of a dish that automatically searches and locks on the satellites and it only takes about fifteen minutes to completely set up dish and receiver. But the setup of the new dish did not go as smooth as it should have. The Dish receiver kept indicating that one satellite input was missing, but there was only one cable from the new satellite dish to the receiver. On top of this the receiver was still set up on programming for Des Moines, Iowa. After spending several hours on Sunday trying to integrate the new satellite dish with the existing Dish receiver, I gave up before becoming completely frustrated. Again, it was Sunday, so of course support for the new dish was closed until Monday.

On Monday I contacted support and found out the satellite dish was not completely compatible with the receiver I have. I would have to run a second cable from the dish to the receiver. As soon as I ran the second cable the receiver recognized the second satellite input. Now our only remaining problems were to contact Dish Network support to have our location set to Las Vegas and download our new program schedule. This took almost an hour and went rather smoothly considering the support person was in India, which is about 13 time zones and two languages away.
Now the second cable runs in the door and across the living room to the receiver. We (I) can live with this until a permanent solution can be worked out, or forever, whichever comes first.

The new dish will eliminate much frustration surrounding setting up the satellite and will probably add ten years to my life and twenty years to Karen's. The big difference between the original manual dish and the new automatic dish is that the new dish would lock on all three satellites at the same time, whereas the old dish could only lock on one at a time. This means that both TV's must be tuned into
programs that are on the same satellite.

****

Computer Things

I had connected all the cabinets, cables, and peripherals on my first installation of a VAX 11780, and it was time to power this baby up. I flipped the power switch on the CPU and the power light came on, but nothing happened. No boot, not output on the console, nothing. I opened the back doors and double checked that the cables were ok, that all the power cables were properly seated when I noticed that none of the fans were spinning. I whipped out my trusty multi meter and confirmed that the fans were getting the correct voltage, but still none of them were spinning. After about 30 minutes of scratching my head, I called support. They had me recheck all cable connections and recheck the input voltage, which I did again with my trusty multi meter. At this point they asked me to double check the input voltage with a scope just in case my trusty $15.00 multi meter was measuring incorrectly. My scope confirmed that the input voltage was correct, but that it was much higher than 60 hertz. On seeing this, the customer knew immediately what the problem was. The electricians had wired the wrong power into the compute room. After the power problem was corrected, I powered up the system and everything ran perfectly, which was great because I was a PDP11 engineer and had no VAX training. Talk about plug and play...

On another occasion I was called to fix a TU45 tape drive that was down. I had been trained on the TU45 two years previously, but the only one in our area had never malfunctioned until now. It was a two-hour drive to the customer's site, so I had plenty of time to attempt to recall what a TU45 looked like and how it worked. On entering the computer room, I powered up the tape drive and nothing happened. I checked the voltages and yes, one was missing. I checked the fuses and yes, one was blown. I replaced the fuse, powered up the drive and everything worked. I powered it up and down and loaded tape half a dozen times to make sure the fuse would not blow again and turned the drive over to the customer. I have been on site 10 minutes and headed back to the office. It took longer to fill out the problem report than it took to fix the problem. My hours of racking my brain on how a TU45 worked were for not...

Another adventure was my supporting an engineer in Kentucky. I drove two hours and arrived about lunch time, so we decided to eat first. Then, since the customer did not have an RK05 diagnostic pack, we borrowed one from another customer. It was about two o'clock by the time we started troubleshooting. The engineer demonstrated how the system crashed. He cut the bus in half by taking a terminator card from his toolbox and inserting it in the middle of the bus, and sure enough the system did not crash. He moved his terminator further down the bus without crashing the system. When he returned the bus to its original configuration it started crashing again. I noticed that when he was troubleshooting, he was using the terminator card from his toolbox and when the system crashed it had the customer's terminator in the last slot. I removed the customer's terminator and sure enough there were several blown resistors. We inserted the engineer's terminator at the end of the bus and the system ran error free. Again, it took almost as long to fill out the LARS report then it took to fix the problem.

I was doing an afterhours installation installing a DH11 on an 11/45 and the customer was helping mount backplanes and install power supplies. When I was ready to test the DH11 I powered up the system and the DH11 smoked. It turned out the customer had crossed some wires from the power supplies to the DH backplane, and I had not checked his work, and a dozen chips had fried. Luckily, the customer was in the chip distribution business. I used my module extender, chip clip and scope to find and replace a dozen fried chips, which the customer supplied. This process took most of the night, but by the start of the next business day the system was up and running and the new DH11 worked perfectly.

****

Unicorn

Sex and sailing are my only remaining vices. I gave up smoking, drinking, and staying out late with the boys when I realized that they were interfering with my sex and sailing. My savings and retirement allowed me to live in relative comfort on my sailboat and savor my simple but enjoyable pleasures.

After working twenty-five years for the agency, I had enough, so on my 45th birthday I took early retirement. I spent my first fifteen years at the agency as an analyst on the European desk. I specialized in East-German/Russian intelligence, but for my last ten years I worked in internal affairs, meaning I spied on the spies. I switched from analyzing foreign intelligence data to investigating agency personnel.

The call from Mike Brewer was an unexpected but welcome intrusion on my relaxing but sometimes unexciting lifestyle. Having retired three years ago, and never having been contacted by my old employer, I knew that the call from Mike saying he would be over in an hour was not a visit to ask my opinion on how the agency should be run. That morning when I saw Mike walking down the pier towards my boat, I knew my retirement was going to be put on hold for a while. I didn't know Mike personally; he was an upper-level manager that I never met, but I knew him by sight and reputation. He was all work and no play and as soon as we got below deck, and before I could even offer him coffee or better yet a beer, he got down to business.

"I don't have enough information to make any accusations or even know who to suspect", but without hesitation he added, "I've come across what looks to be a conspiracy to assassinate the President." "Why not keep this internal? Why rummage through the retirement role? I asked. "I've enough small pieces of information to give me a strong feeling that somebody inside and close to the top is heading the attempt. The only person I can trust is an outsider or somebody that has been outside for the past few years that, and your well-known admiration for President Kennedy were the deciding factors in my selecting you." He handed me a one-page file with a newspaper picture attached. "The only information I have makes this guy our assassin, so I need you to check on him. His code name is Unicorn. He defected to Russia, married a Russian girl and after a few years became disenchanted with the Russian lifestyle and he returned to the United States with his new bride. I need to know what he's up to and I need to know within two days."

Mike handed me an envelope which contained $2,000 in $100 bills, a business card with his private phone number on one side, a phone number and password written on the other side, and my old identification card. "I'll be at that number every day from 2330 until 2345. The other number is a dial in line to our computer network and the password to an untraceable highly privileged account. Do not contact any of your old friends at the agency for information on this. The only thing I can say is to be careful and work alone. Do you have any questions?" Since I did not have any questions, and he had finished, Mike got up and left.

As soon as Mike left, I went to the local library to see what information was available on Unicorn. Dialing into the agency computer, I found Oswld's file which contained information on several recent trips to Mexico and a visit to the Russian embassy, that he was an ex-marine and he and his wife were living in Dallas. The information I found indicated that someone at the agency was keeping close tabs on Oswald. I found that he was active in the Cuban Liberation Front, CLF. His file indicated that he had made several overnight visits to Mexico City and his last trip was for three nights. In the circles I ran in, Mexico City, like Vienna, had a reputation as being a "spy city". The Russians meet operatives and conduct business there just as if they were at home. During these visits, the Centro Nacional de Inteligencia (CNI), which is the Mexican equivalent to the CIA. During his three-day visit he was observed entering the Russian Embassy. Why was the CNI keeping an eye on Oswald? Who at the agency had requested the surveillance? I then hacked into the credit bureau computers. From this I found that Unicorn had a Master card and a Visa card, so much for computer security. In checking both accounts, the Master Card showed nothing, but the Visa card showed he'd charged the room for each of his one-night visits, but nothing for the recent three-day visit. Where did he stay for his three-night stay? Just to cover all the bases, I checked Oswald's file on the FBI and Secret Service computers. Both systems had only the basic information but nothing about his support of the CLF and the trips to Mexico. Why was the agency not sharing intelligence about Oswald's support of the CLF and more disturbing was way was the agency withholding investigative evidence of a potential domestic terrorist activity?

I caught the next as to Dallas. A check of the Dallas police computer showed that he had lived in the area for the past three years, worked for the city, was still married, and had no police record. His file was marked 'POLITICAL' He'd been observed on several occasions handing out leaflets and demonstrating in support of Castro and Cuba while denouncing the U.S. isolation policy towards Cuba.

I made a visit to the Dallas Police Political Section and showed the duty Sgt my almost valid identification card. "The only thing I have is confirmation of his association with the CLF, that's the Cuban Liberation Front." he told me. "Great, that doesn't give me any more than I already have." "I can tell you that the CLF is angry at Kennedy for giving the CIA the go ahead to assassinate Castro and for the Bay of Pigs. They said that if anything happens to Castro, Kennedy would be assassinated. We don't have any information that they've taken any action in carrying out this threat."

He then added in a pleading tone, "I've been working in the Political group for three years and I'm starting to vegetate. We investigate, report, investigate, report and nothing comes of it. Can you put in a good word for me with your boss and tell him I'm interested in working for your organization?" "Sure, I'll put in a good word for you." In the older days I would have given him the name of the surveillance group supervisor. Surveillance means bad hours, bad pay, and disgusting food. Sometimes you should be satisfied with what you have. The biggest problem with life is knowing when to hold 'em!!

"Why are you guys checking Oswald's' background again so soon? " He asked.

"What do you mean?" I asked inquisitively.

"It's only been about two weeks since someone from your organization was in here asking similar questions about this guy."

"He was probably from a different section and our investigations are overlapping. Do you remember who the last guy was?

"Yea, I've got his business card right here in my drawer."

"Here it is." he said handing me the card on which identified the bearer as 'Steve Sims - Senior Investigator – Central Intelligence Agency - United States of America.

"He's not in my section. I'll check and see why we're both are doing a background investigation of the same person."

I remember Steve Sims. I had a few run ins with him over the years. He was a right-wing a hole. His way was the only way. I was surprised that he'd lasted this long with the agency. He must have a guardian angel looking out for him. I thanked the sergeant and went out to find something to eat.

Since I was on expenses, I found a sea food place and consumed my weight in peel and ate shrimp and savored my one beer.

Nowadays one of the few places you can go and spend a couple of hours without savoring an alcoholic drink is a movie theater or a library, I opted for the library where I read for a few hours while waiting to call Mike.

I found a payphone and updated Mike on today's findings. "Follow up on the visits to Mexico. Sounds like a training trip to me. See if he is taking a trip in the next few days. Watch out for Sims. I am not surprised he is connected to the CLF. Talk to you tomorrow." And with that the line went dead.

Early the next morning I went to see Unicorn's employer. "This is highly confidential, and nothing is to be said about this visit to the person under discussion. If you understand this, please sign the form." The form signing gets them every time. "What can you tell me about his

"Nothing, he's a loner and doesn't talk much to anyone." Was the answer I got back.

"Has he been absent from work much?"

"Other than vacation he hasn't missed any work. He does take a one- or two-day vacation regularly, but he gives at least two weeks' notice before taking it."

"Has he scheduled any vacation in the next two weeks?"

"Let me see." he said while searching through some papers. "Yes, He scheduled three days starting today. Anything else?" he asked.

"Anything you want to add to your statement?" I asked in an official tone.

"No, nothing I can think of," he answered.

"Please remember the confidentiality of this meeting." I added as I left.

I needed to get on a computer to check some things out, so I made a visit to the local library. Using the number and password Mike gave me, I logged into the agency's system. The first thing I checked was the charge cards. Nothing. I checked the airline reservation computers and they showed that he made a flight yesterday, but the itinerary was strange. He had reservations from Dallas to Boston to Washington DC to Atlanta then back to Dallas. In each city except Atlanta, he had at least a 12-hour layover. I checked a couple of the hotel reservation systems and found that he had reservations at the Holiday Inn in Boston, but not in any of the other cities. I checked his file at the agency and found the same thing that I had found at the library. Someone had either laundered the file, or the administrative function had broken down when it came to keep this file updated. In my years at the agency, I'd only seen a one admin screw up and this didn't feel like one.

I went out and called Mike from a payphone. I tried three times between 2330 and 2345, but no answer. Something was wrong. As important as this was, Mike wouldn't miss a contact. I had to trust someone, so I called Cheryl. I have known her for the past 15 years. We lived together for five years and almost got married a few years ago. If I had to trust anyone it had to be her.

"Hi Cheryl, this is John Davis. How have you been?" I asked. This was a way to let her recognize my voice and let her know not to say my real name. "Great John, how are you? It has been over a month since I last heard from you. What've you been doing?" she replied.

"I've been really busy. What I called for was to see if you were busy tomorrow?

"I have to work" She started to say something else when I cut her off with, "Hey, I see my bus. Call me at home later and we can talk." And I hung up.

Within 30 minutes of getting home, Cheryl called "Do you know what time it is? "She teasingly asked. "I left my warm cozy bed to find a phone booth to return your call." She stated tauntingly.

"Thanks Cheryl, I didn't know who else to trust. Do you know Mike Brewer?"

"What the hell is going on? You haven't called for over a month. Then you call in the middle of the night asking if I know someone who just happens to have died yesterday." Her voice changed to a questioning worried tone when she asked, "Now I suppose you're going to tell me it wasn't a heart attack."

"That's right; I don't think he died of a natural cause. What do you know about Mike?"

"Not much, I never worked for him. He didn't talk much, I liked him. Not much I can tell you."

"I need a big favor. I need you to check on what Steve Sims is working on and where he is now. Be careful and don't let anyone know what you're doing. I'll be at 617-555-1212 so call me about ten tomorrow morning. Thanks. "After hanging up I found myself in the middle of a flashback of the relationship and great times we had shared over the years. I would have to rethink our relationship and take it to the next step, MARRIAGE. I would have to think this through when I had more time. Definitely not something to decide on the spur of the moment.

I caught the next flight to Boston and on arrival went directly to the Holiday Inn and checked in. I showed the bell captain Unicorn's picture. "This guy checked in a couple hours ago, but I haven't really seen him since." He said.

I left him my room number and a $20.00 bill telling him that if he spotted my man and called me there would be an additional $50 in it for him. Money is a good motivator and don't let anyone tell you different. I picked up the local paper and went to my room to read and try and get a few hours' sleep. On the front page of the paper was a picture of the President and a story telling how he'd be in a parade tomorrow. Inside the paper was a map of the parade route and the times he'd be in various locations on the route.

My priority was to stop Unicorn and the second was to ensure he was never able to try this again. The first part should be easy to accomplish. For the second I'd must either kill him or turn him over to the police and somehow get them to understand how I knew what his intentions were. Killing him was the surest way to ensure he never had another opportunity to try this again. Now I needed a way to do it while keeping myself from going to jail for his murder. Killing him had to be done away from the hotel because too many people had seen me there.

The phone woke me up at 6 a.m. the next morning.

"This is the bell captain. Your man has just gone up to his room."

"Thanks, I'll be down in 15 minutes," I said as I was getting dressed.

As I approached the Bell Captain's Station, rushed out to meet me in anticipation of his $50 reward. "He got out of a cab, picked up his key and went to his room," he said frantically.

"Do you know the cab number or the cab company?"

"I can do better than that, I know the cab driver," he said. "Let me get his work number for you." He walked over to his station.

I called the number and left a message for the driver to call me immediately. He called 20 minutes later.

"Thanks for calling. Where did you pick up the man you dropped off at the Holiday Inn about 30 minutes ago?"

"Let's see. I picked him up in front of the building at Charles and River Street."

"Did you notice where he came from before you picked him up?"

"Yea, he came out of the book depository on River Street." he answered.

"Did he have a box or case with him?" I asked.

"No, nothing"

"Thanks. The bell captain at the Holiday Inn will have a $20 bill for you."

I checked the location of the book depository with relation to the President's route and the President's motorcade would be going right in front of the depositary at exactly 2 P.M. this afternoon. I need to check out the inside of that building now.

I arrived at the depository 20 minutes later and got inside with no problems. This was going to be easier than I thought. Nobody even asked what I was doing. After spending a couple of hours checking out the windows facing the street on the top four floors, I still didn't have the correct floor or window identified, but at least I was now extremely familiar with those four floors. If it were this easy for me to gain access to any part of the building, an assassin would have the same freedom of movement.

I only had a few hours to stop Unicorn's assignation attempt on President Kennedy. I'd come back to the building an hour prior to the President's motorcade would be passing by and take care of Unicorn then. I headed back to the hotel.

The doorman acted like my long-lost brother. He pulled me aside to tell me that the guy I was looking for had checked out about an hour ago.

"Did he have any luggage when he checked out?" I asked.

"Just a small overnight bag."

"Did he take a cab when he left?"

"No. He just walked away." I slipped the doorman his $50 and he took me to Unicorn's vacant room and let me in. He left me alone. I checked everything and every place and found nothing.

Since he had only one small bag when he arrived and left, the weapon must already be stashed someplace, or he went out to buy one, or someone had one ready for him. I checked the room a second time and again came up with nothing.

I went to my room, called room service, and ordered some sandwiches and lots of coffee and I waited for the call from Cheryl. She called at exactly ten. "That matter you wanted me to check on left town last night for parts unknown. Whatever he's working on I can't find out what it is or who it's for. From what I've heard you don't want to cross this guy or turn your back on him. Sorry I couldn't be of any more help to you."

"Thanks Cheryl, I'll call you in a day or two and we can talk over old times. Be careful." With that I hung up.

I got back to the book depository as quickly as possible. I put on my gloves to keep from leaving my fingerprints everywhere. After checking floors four through seven and finding them all empty. I stationed myself in a cleaning room on the fourth floor between the stairs and elevator. I propped open the door so I could hear anyone climbing the stairs. The only problem with my plan came from all the coffee I'd drank earlier. The bathrooms were at the other end of the building and Unicorn could slip past me while I was gone. Fortunately, cleaning the closet sink solved my problem.

After waiting for two and a half hours, and several trips to the cleaning closet, I heard the elevator startup. I positioned myself in the cleaning closet and waited. This had to be the slowest moving elevator in the northern hemisphere. It finally bypassed my floor, continued, and then stopped, but I had no way of knowing which floor it stopped on. Given the amount of time it took to get from the first floor to the fourth floor, it didn't have time to get to the seventh floor meaning it was either on five or six. Both five and six were used as storage areas and were filled with boxes with the aisles leading to the row of windows across the front of the building. With less than thirty minutes to go I headed for the stairs to the fifth floor. In this old building the floors and stairs were made of wood and every step caused them to creak and groan and it was making the hair on my arms stand up. Not that I had much hair on my arms. I moved slowly to make as little noise as possible. I finally got to the door leading to the fifth floor. If he had gone to the window, he wouldn't be able to see the door leading to the stairs, so, I opened it slowly. Luckily, the door didn't creak, and I slipped onto the fifth floor quietly closing the door behind me. I slowly moved towards the front of the building and towards the windows. On this floor you could see the whole line of windows. This meant that when I looked down the row of windows, I'd be able to see him and that he'd be able to see me. I got out my gun and screwed on the silencer. If I had to shoot, I didn't want to attract too much attention. I made my way to one the far end of the room so that I only had to look in one direction and would get a quick view of all the windows at one time. The easy part was getting there, the hard part was mustering the courage to stick my head out in an exposed position and see if I could see a man with a rifle and at the same time hope that he didn't see me. I decided that a crouched position, with my head near the floor, peeking around the corner of a box was the least exposed position and if need be, I was in a good position to get a shot at him. Cautiously I inched my way to the edge of the box and peeked around the corner. It felt like I was watching a movie instead of being a participant in the drama. Slowly the aisle came into view a few feet at a time, so far nothing. At least he wasn't standing right next to me. After what seemed like minutes but was only seconds. I had a full view of all the windows, and nothing. I could feel my body sag in relief and tense again when I realized that I'd have to climb another flight of stairs and go through the whole thing again. I now had less than twenty minutes and had to move a little faster. I made my way back to the stairs and up to the door to the sixth floor. I held my breath and with the gun in front of me I slowly opened the door. It was like a movie again; the hallway came gradually into view foot by foot until I could see it was empty. I moved into the hallway and closed the door behind me. I followed the same route as on the floor below and inched my way toward the window aisle. I could feel my heart beating in my chest, and I could hear it pounding in my ears. As I slowly inched my head around the corner of the boxes the aisle again came gradually into view foot by foot until I saw him.

As soon as I saw someone in the aisle my heart began pounding even harder and my body began shaking. I pulled back behind the box so I could regain control. I made myself count to ten and I slowly moved out into the aisle with my gun in the ready position.

SHIT!!! There were two of them. I'd already committed myself and now I was facing two bad guys instead of one. In a half state of shock, I think I said "freeze", but I was too slow. One of them was swinging a rifle barrel in my direction. I pulled off three quick shots and both went down hard. With any luck they were both dead and I could walk away clean. After waiting several minutes to see if anyone moved, which was only about ten seconds, I slowly moved down the aisle. I needed to ensure that one of them was Unicorn and see if the other one was Sims. About halfway down the aisle, I noticed out the window that the President's motorcade had passed by the building, and he was now out of danger. As I started down the aisle again, I heard a noise behind me. As I turned to check, my head exploded, my legs went limp, and the world went black. My last recognizable thought was, "SHIT" there are three of them!!! "

I woke up to the smell of gasoline and smoke. I felt the heat of the fire. I could hear the shrill sound of the smoke alarm. It took me a full six seconds to realize that I had to get out of there before the fire department came and started asking unanswerable questions. I got about ten feet before I remembered my gun. I crawled back and found it and headed for the stairs. I listened at the door to the stairway to ensure no one was coming up. I quickly ducked into the stairway and headed down. I got as far as the fourth floor before I heard people coming up the stairs. I quickly left the stairwell and headed for the fire escape outside the back of the building. I made it out the window and down the fire escape without being seen. I dropped my gun in the first trashcan I saw. As I was walking away from the building, I felt my legs starting to get rubbery and my vision starting to blur. I made it four blocks before I had to sit down on the curb for a few minutes to let my body return to normal after being abused by that guy on the sixth floor.

The next thing I remember is a scene from a "B" movie where the guy opens his eyes, and everything is out of focus. As things begin to clear a light comes into view and sure enough the scene is taking place in a hospital room, and I am playing the lead. And just like in the movies I don't remember anything between sitting down to rest and waking up here. In looking around the room I can see that I hadn't been carrying my medical insurance card because I'd guess by the sparse surroundings that I am in a state funded hospital. I get out of bed slowly. I feel ok, but I won't be moving fast for a few days. I felt a little exposed, so I put on a robe and started down the hall. I see a cluster of nurses at the nurses' station, so I head for them. As I got closer, I noticed that they were watching television and several of them are crying. I asked the nearest nurse what was going on, and she said, "The President was shot and killed a few hours ago!"

"Impossible, I saw his car go by the window and he was ok!" I exclaimed loudly.

"You've been in the hospital for the past two days. You must've seen the President when he was here in Boston two days ago. He was assassinated a few hours ago in Dallas by a man named Oswald."

"Shit", I said under my breath "Unicorn was, the third man."

****

Snakes on the Train

My harrowing adventure started on a normal summer day in the Adventure Place amusement park. I was the operator, engineer, of the amusement park train. The A-Train consists of a diesel locomotive pulling five passenger cars which seat up to fourteen passengers each. The cars have open sides and a metal roof which attempts to shield the passengers from the sun and rain, but since the sides are open the shielding from the sun is only effective at noon and any protection from the rain is only effective when there is no wind. The locomotive engineer's comforts are a different story. He has no roof and therefore no protection from the elements.

First let me clear up a misconception you may be under concerning the title of this story. I hate snakes; therefore, there are no snakes in this story. With the recent deluge of snake stories, I thought the title was an attention grabber and would attract readers to at least start reading the story.

On leaving the station one Saturday afternoon with a full load of seventy passengers and one crew, unbeknownst to me four suspected terrorists in the last car climbed on the roof and proceeded to make their way to the front of the train. Just like in the movies they ran along the roof and jumped over the crevasse between the cars. Due to bad planning on their part, they were unaware that within two hundred yards of leaving the station the train entered a low clearance tunnel. The first terrorist saw the tunnel and dropped down and laid flat on the roof. He was the lucky one; the remaining terrorists were scrapped off the roof like frosting off a cake. No, that is not a very good metaphor. Like a child scraping the frosting off a cake, that seems better.

After exiting the tunnel, the lone remaining terrorist resumed his trek towards the engine. He jumped onto the seat beside me and announced that the train was now in his control and that he wanted me to crash the A-Train into the Ferris wheel. I politely pointed out to this imbecile that the train could only go where the tracks were and that the tracks were not near enough to allow me to crash the train into the Ferris wheel. Thinking quickly, as train engineers sometimes do, I told him that there was an old, abandoned track that led directly to the Amusement Parks Roller Coaster Control Center and that this would cause far more damage than crashing into the Ferris wheel. He reluctantly agreed but said that he would cause me great bodily harm if I tried anything funny. I headed the train towards the bridge over the lake, as if I had any recourse because that's where the tracks went. My plan was simple, when the train got in the middle of the bridge over the lake, I would push the terrorist off the engine, and he would plummet down three feet into the lake as I sped off into the sunset. My plan went great, but the terrorist made a really horrific mistake. Thinking he was an Olympic diver he attempted to make a perfect entry into the water with his arms extended over his head, his legs together and his body straight as a rail. In an Olympic pool he would have received a 9 or 10 for his diving attempt, but in the lake, he received two broken arms and a slight concussion because the water was only eighteen inches deep.

I was to learn later that two of the terrorists were actually FAPTM (Federal Amusement Park Train Marshals) and they were attempting to apprehend the two terrorists when they were unceremoniously scrapped off the roof of the train with one of the terrorists. I wasn't aware of the highly secret Amusement Park Marshal program. They are highly trained Marshals with specialties such as Bumper Car Marshals, Ferris wheel Marshals and the infamous Roller Coaster Marshals to name the less classified specialties of the Amusement Park Marshal program. They were paid to ride all of the rides in the Amusement Park and be ever vigilant for any possible terrorist activities. In a still highly classified document, the FAPTM program is credited with quashing a plot to take control of the Bumper cars at Disneyland and rain havoc on the Los Angeles freeways. The terrorist's plan was to commandeer the amusement parks bumper cars. They planned on infiltrating a crack parachute combat team onto the sky ride and parachute into the roof of the bumper car building. They then planned to drive the bumper cars onto the freeway bumping into cars in an attempt to induce road rage which would increase the amount of havoc they could reap. More than just raising havoc and causing chaos on the Los Angeles freeways, above and beyond the normal havoc and chaos, a vital objective of this operation was to raise money for the terrorist coffers. The terrorist organization had secretly purchased hundreds of body repair shops in the Los Angeles area and planned to gouge the insurance companies on the repairs.

In its infinite wisdom, the Justice Department's Witness Protection Program took over the body repair shops that were confiscated from the terrorists and placed hundreds of protected witnesses as operators of these body shops. The object was to place these protected people in a position to earn a living and provide a service to the community. In reality what occurred was exactly the same thing that the terrorists had planned, the new operators gouged the insurance companies and local authorities could not prosecute them because they were protected by the Justice Department.

****

Walking the (Alien) Dog

In 1993 an amazing discovery was made during the excavation of Outlaw Gulch. What looked like an experimental aircraft was discovered buried 20 feet underground. The fact that it was an aircraft was not the amazing part because the land which Adventureland now occupies was the Altoona Airport back in the 1920's, in fact Charles Lindberg landed at the airport in 1927. The Federal Aviation Agency was notified, and the story ends with the FAA removing the craft, which was never heard of again, until:

A thirteen-year-old schoolgirl from Clear Lake, Iowa, whose father had worked on building Outlaw Gulch and had told her the story of the discovery of the aircraft that had been taken away and never heard from again, received a reply from the FAA regarding a freedom of information action she had submitted when she was eleven years old. Just two weeks ago, an underpaid overworked FAA clerk found the request and noted that it was several years old, so he processed it and sent the girl the following account.

The amazing part of the discovery is the speed at which the Federal Aviation Agency responded to the discovery and the speed with which they removed the newly discovered craft. Within hours it was unearthed, packed and air lifted to Nellis Air Force Base near Las Vegas, Nevada.

The only problem is that the craft never arrived at Nellis; it was spirited off the top secret, nonexistent, facility north of Las Vegas affectionately known as Area 51.

The reason the FAA moved so fast in removing the aircraft was that when they examined the interior of the craft, they discovered a living alien life form.

Upon arriving at Area 51, the life form was examined, studied, poked, and prodded for the next nineteen years. The composition of its body was translucent like that of a jellyfish. This was good news for the alien life form. Since its internal organs were visible, they did not have to cut it open to determine how it worked. Unlike the aircraft which for the next nineteen years was taken apart, tested, and reassembled dozens of times.

The doctor heading the examination of the alien life form named it Bernadette. He chose Bernadette because he had a crush on Bernadette Peters and his DVD library contained every movie she had made, all 32 of them. Since Bernadette is a feminine name, Bernadette was referred to as her or she from then on, although, much like a worm, she could reproduce any time she wanted. During the nineteen-year examination period she must have had one continues headache because she/he never reproduced.

After the doctors spent several months examining Bernadette, they became sickened at the constant sight of her internal organs, and they pitched in and bought her a Halloween costume to wear. As chance would have it the only Halloween costume available in Las Vegas in June was a dog costume.

In 2002 it was decided that there must have been a compelling reason that Bernadette had landed in Altoona, so they made plans to relocate her back to Iowa. The thought was that if Bernadette were back in Altoona, her alien companions would attempt to contact her, and they could then be identified and monitored. Since the spot where Bernadette had landed was now an amusement park, it was decided to let her wear the dog costume and get her a job as the park mascot. The only problem was that the park wanted a masculine name, so Bernadette was renamed Bernie.

In an attempt to identify Bernie's alien companions, the Federal Amusement Park Marshal's provided agents to accompany Bernie everywhere he went. They referred to this duty as "Walking the Dog".

Over the years they have reported that many really strange people had made contact with Bernie, but none could be identified as aliens.

****

The Origins of the Federal Amusement Park Marshals Service (FAPMS)

In January 1977, then President Gerald Ford had a dream, not a nightmare, not about pardoning Nixon or falling down the steps of Air Force One on national television, but of terrorist wreaking havoc on the nation's amusement parks. Before he could act on his nightmare, he was out of office and Jimmy Carter was in.

During Presidents Carter's presidency he had too many real-life nightmares to deal with, so he didn't dare dream.

In July 1988, President Reagan was in his seventh year as President when he started having nightmares, no not about the soundness of his "trickle-down" economic theory, but his recurring nightmare was concerning terrorist causing mayhem in the nation's amusement parks.

Since the subject of the "trickle-down" theory was broached, I personally do not subscribe to that particular theory. Why give rich people more money and hope it trickles down to the less advantaged? Why not put the money where it is needed and give it directly to the less advantaged, who in turn will spend it on the products and services they need most, which will give the manufactures incentive to provide the products which the less advantaged are purchasing thereby enabling them to expand and hire more employees. I have labeled this the "bubble-up" economic theory, but then who is going to listen to someone who writes short stories and is a charter member of the less advantaged class…

After enduring several months of nightmarish terrorist dreams, President Reagan took action. He wanted to assign someone to assess the potential damage that that terrorist could cause in the nation's amusement parks. He deliberated for weeks over who could be trusted with the assignment until he finally broke down and asked Nancy who she would recommend. With his selection decided for him, he proceeded to brief the new head of Amusement Park Security on assessing the threat and developing a plan to counter that threat.

After an exhaustive one-year investigation in which every amusement park in the country was visited and every ride was ridden, it was determined that the terrorist threat was extremely high, and the plan called for the formation of a marshal's service to protect the parks. It was also determined that this should be a highly classified program because of the potential loss of business due to the public's reaction to a possible terrorist attack within the parks. It was also decided that the headquarters and training facility would be in a small out of the way park, of which Adventureland was selected.

While the park was closed during the winter of 1990, a secret underground facility was excavated beneath the Iowa Farm section of the park. Prior to the parks opening in April the rides and buildings were replaced to their original positions and on opening day it looked like nothing had changed. The inconspicuous entrance to the new facility was through the Big Pig. If you are familiar with the pig, you know the entrance is through the pig's rear end.

The point of entry was the *butt* of many jokes and the FAPMS management finally had enough of the jokes so during the week when the park was closed, the entrance was moved to the River Rapids Log Flume better known as the Log Ride. The marshals would be carried on the log ride like any other park visitor and the log would then be diverted to the secret entrance to the underground facility.

There turned out to be two problems with this decision. First during peak ride times, it took the marshals up to an hour of waiting in line to get on the log ride and they then complained about getting drenched and having to wear wet clothing all day…

The next week the park was closed so the entrance was moved to the Silly Silo, but the ride made so many marshals sick that within a few days the entrance was moved back to the log ride. Moving the entrance to the Outlaw, the Dragon and the Sky Ride were quickly dismissed due to many marshals having Acrophobia, a fear of heights. This left the area now occupied by the Underground as the only alternative so during the week that the park was closed a tunnel was dug to the secret underground facility and the entrance was moved to the area near the Underground. When the Underground was eventually built in 1996, the connecting tunnel was extended between the rides exit and secret facility under the Iowa Farm section, where it remains to this day. As you enter the exit to the Underground ride you go through the first door on the right that reads "Employees Only", you then encounter the security shack where you must pass the retinal scan, the palm print scan and the facial recognition scan. Once you have successfully passed these identification stations you can enter the elevator which takes you down to the marshals' facility.

Now that they had the housekeeping function out of the way they got down to training the marshals. The marshal organization was set up similar to the park organization with the following training sections; rides, games, food service, security with the added category of patrons (park visitors). In the amusement park business, it only takes hours to train the people in their specialty, in the marshal service it took weeks to train the government employees to the same degree. Not that the training was any more in depth, it provided outstanding customer service that was the hardest concept to get across to the new government employees.

Once the marshals graduated, their assignment was to inconspicuously enter an assigned amusement park, ride the rides, play the games, eat the food and be ever vigilant for possible terrorist activates.

To trim expenses the government negotiated a free parking deal with the various amusement parks. Each marshal was given a sticker for the windshield of his/her car which granted them free parking. Pictured on the sticker was a rear view of the original entrance to the secret underground training facility (the pig).

A tat recognition system was implemented at all parks in early 2005. Every person entering the park with a tattoo had their tat photographed and the picture run though the Tat recognition computer to see if they are on the national watch list. Many false arrest lawsuits were filed because no one in the government had considered that multiple people can be adorned with the same tat and the computer went wild when these popular tats were encountered. This project was cancelled within weeks of its implementation.

Soon after the tat fiasco, a facial recognition system was implemented. During the initial trials it was found that all older men with full heavy beards were identified as Fidel Castro, and all young thin blond women were identified as Paris Hilton. In the first case the FBI was notified and in the second the paparazzi were alerted. The paparazzi complained so vehemently about the false notifications on Paris Hilton sightings that the system was taken offline until the bugs could be worked out.

Following the idea behind the airline's no-fly list, a no-ride list was implemented. To test the effectiveness of the no-ride list and the facial recognition system, a sting operation was implemented with the FAPMS mailing out 100,000 letters to suspected terrorists and wanted felons informing them that they had won a season pass to their local amusement park. The only thing they had to do was show up at the park and pick up their season pass. When they arrived, they were photographed, presumably for their pass. While they were waiting, the pictures were run through the facial recognition program and the person's name was compared to the no-ride list. If either one got a hit the felons were arrested, and the terrorists placed under surveillance. During the thirty-day test ten terrorists and ninety-five wanted felons were arrested at a cost of over twenty-five million dollars. It was later discovered that the mailing list used in the sting was of 100,000 postal workers and the FAPMS was charged for 99,895 season passes for the postal workers not caught in the sting. The FAPMS vehemently defends its stance that the sting was a success because it validated the facial recognition and no-ride databases, but congress was not buying it and declared that the FAPMS was NEVER to attempt another sting operation.

What the FAPMS did not tell congress is that they had obtained the cell phone numbers of the terrorists identified during the sting. The expectation being that they could track the terrorists' movements which would lead them to discover the sleeper cells associated with each terrorist.

Since the FAPMS was a highly secret agency, its' hiring practices were not hindered by any government oversight, meaning the agency hired many relatives and friends of senior managers. In some cases, this was ok because the people were competent in the areas in which they were assigned. But in several critical areas, such as entry level clerical workers, any applicant recommended by a senior manager was instantly hired. After the damage was done, it was found that several of the clerical workers had not graduated from high school, could not read at a sixth-grade level and none knew how to type. When they were assigned the task of keying in the information of the terrorists identified in the season pass sting into the GPS tracking system, they made several critical mistakes that once again would embarrass the agency.

One of the most publicized mistakes that an entry level clerical worker made was that instead of entering a terrorist's name as Shalala Pala he mistakenly entered Sarah Palin, and since the clerk forgot to enter the cell phone number, the system queried the national cell phone database and entered Sarah's actual cell number. Since all terrorists were assigned code names, Shalala Pala was assigned the code name of Maverick, the significance of which was not discovered until much later. When they started scrutinizing the travel information collected by the GPS system, they found that Maverick was traveling freely within all fifty states which lead them to believe they had uncovered a senior terrorist leader who was visiting sleeper cells across the country. When Maverick was tracked to Washington D.C., they decided that this was getting to close to critical government targets, and they raided Maverick Washington D.C. location.

Maverick was traced to the ballroom at the InterContinental Hotel The Willard Washington D.C. on Pennsylvania Avenue Northwest only few blocks from the White House. When they entered the hotel and discovered that the Republican National Committee was meeting in the ballroom, they panicked. They assumed the terrorists were going to use saran gas or some such device to eliminate the entire senior leadership of the Republican Party. They immediately notified the FBI, Homeland Security, the CIA, the Washington Police, the Washington Fire Department and, in hopes of gaining some much-needed positive publicity, they notified the Washington Post. Within minutes the InterContinental Willard Hotel was surrounded by hundreds of uniformed police and firemen, and hundreds of men and women in suits of various colors and styles from thirty government agencies. When the handheld Garmin cell phone Global Positioning System led them to Sarah Palin's purse it should have given them some indication that things were not what they seemed, but it took them several more hours and hundreds of strip searches to realize the faux pas that had taken place.

Congress was not as lenient this time; they called on President Obama to immediately replace the head of the FAPMS and unequivocally stated that any new head of that organization must obtain prior congressional approval. Before the President could fire the head of the FAPMS he resigned and went to work for British Petroleum as the Vice President in charge of well safety.

President Obama agonized for weeks trying to find a person that could not only do the job but would also be approved by congress. Finally, he asked Michele who she thought would be an acceptable head for the FAPMS. Following in President Reagan footsteps, President Obama accepted Michele's suggestion and submitted the name of Chelsea Clinton to congress as the new head of the FAPMS. No one wanted to tangle with either one of the Clintons, so in secret hearings Chelsea was unanimously approved by both houses of congress as the new head of the Federal Amusement Park Marshals Service.

****

In early 2005, the pentagon realized that the way they evaluated potential recruits was not getting the job done as they were having too many recruits being discharged for various reasons during the first six months of active duty.

After more than a dozen special investigations and hundreds of suggested changes, the following was decided; all potential recruits must attend an intensive four-week mental, physical and stress evaluation period.

At this point it took another dozen special boards to determine what would constitute the curriculum of this four-week period.

Due to heavy budget cuts, very little money was available to build a special evaluation facility, so it was decided to lease a suitable location. After several heated discussions, the sites were narrowed down to two locations: Camp Pendleton, California and Lackland Air Force Base, Texas.

Since consensus could not be reached on which site to use, Defense Secretary Gates, as all great men seem to do, asked his wife Becky as to which location she thought would make a suitable evaluation center.

Taking her suggestion, Secretary Gates broke the deadlock by selecting medium sized amusement park in Iowa as the recruit evaluation site.

The curriculum was as follows:

Their navigation skills were tested by having them plot a course for the log ride boats from the start of the ride to the finish without getting lost. If they failed, they were earmarked for Navy officer's candidate training.

Their tolerance to pain was tested by having them hold on to a rope and being towed around the entire course of the log ride. If they released the rope prior to traversing the first conveyer belt, it was determined that their tolerance for pain was very low, so they were assigned to dental hygienists. If they were released prior to reaching the top of the high conveyer, they were determined to be smart enough to avoid pain and of medium intellect and were assigned to Military Intelligence. If the completed the course by holding on to the rope down the high conveyer slide, they were classified as having an extremely high tolerance to pain and low intellect and were therefore assigned as the legal offices as lawyers.

Their ability to follow orders was tested on the various rides. On the roller coaster rides they were instructed not to pull down on the overhead safety bars, on the sky ride they were instructed to quickly exit to the left, on various rides they were repeatedly told that no personal items can be left behind, they were told that there was no smoking in the park, and they were told that you must meet the height requirements on all tides. Even after being told over and over of the above instructions' forty-five percent did not follow the instructions and were thus assigned to various services budgeting offices as budget analysts.

****

Thoughts from Iowa

The bad news from Iowa is that the weather has been 90-95 degrees with the humidity has also been 90-95 percent. The good news from Iowa is that the women here have been dressing appropriately or inappropriately depending on your outlook.

I have come to the conclusion that I may not revive my beard.

Over the years I have invested too much time and money in sculpturing my facial features.

It has taken 82 years of living, 60 years of marriage, a lot of good wine, more good beer, some great single malt scotch, tons of good food, some bad women, some good women, four children and six grandchildren to create the facial features I display to the world, why hide all that effort behind a beard?

****

The Iowa Sweet Corn Conspiracy

This story is unfolding as we speak, or more aptly, as you read.

The story began innocently enough with a "Freedom of Information" request from a ten-year-old girl from Pella, Iowa for a Social Studies school project. Let me clarify her age, she was ten years old when she submitted the proper request to the Department of Agriculture in February of 2007, and she was twelve in June of 2009 when she received the information she had requested. Consequently, she had received a "D" in Social Studies in 2007 for not submitting her assigned agriculture report. This grade would have a profound impact on the direction her life would take, but that is a different story for another time.

Her request was simple but somewhat naive: "What is the worst secret bad thing that the Department of Agriculture is doing?"

The reason it took over two years to respond to the request was the word "worst". The decision on which was the "worst" bad thing went not only to the highest levels of the Department of Agriculture, but also the Department of Justice, the US Government Accountability Office, The Corp of Engineers, and a score of unnamed secret agencies. It took these bureaucratic entities over two years to determine which bad thing was the "worst" bad thing they were doing. In June of 2009, a gargantuan mistake was made by a low level overworked underpaid paper pushing employee. In an attempt to clear the backlog of Freedom of Information requests an order went out to immediately process all requests over two years old. One week later the now twelve-year-old girl received the classified documentation describing the "worst bad thing", which has aptly been named "The Iowa Sweet Corn Conspiracy".

The "The Iowa Sweet Corn Conspiracy" began thirty years ago when it was determined the program to convert corn to ethanol would eventually consume all of Iowa's yearly corn production leaving no Iowa Sweet Corn for human consumption. A secret government study found that the people of the mid-west would not tolerate a summer without Iowa Sweet Corn. Can you imagine an Iowa family barbeque without Iowa Sweet Corn? The Iowa State Fair would not be the same without roasted Iowa Sweet Corn saturated with butter and sprinkled heavily with salt and what about the unemployed tens of thousands of Iowans who would normally be selling Iowa Sweet Corn out of their pickups?

A secret covert operation was devised to smuggle Missouri corn into Iowa and pass it off as Iowa Sweet Corn. To gain acceptance in Missouri the US Government would smuggle Iowa grape extract into Missouri. The reason that Iowa grape extract was chosen is that the fledgling Missouri wine growers needed a high-quality grape to combine with the native Missouri grape, but it would take years of breading and cross breading grapes to obtain the high-quality grape required. The Iowa grape was an excellent grape to combine with the Missouri grape to create a high quality "Missouri" wine.

To implement the smuggling operation an amusement park was built to house the Iowa end of the operation. The focal point of the amusement park project was the underground gold my ride. While digging the tunnels for the ride, one train tunnel was extended 360 miles to Hermann, Missouri, which is in the heart of the Missouri wine trail. The construction of the tunnel went unnoticed because it was thought to be improvements to the interstate highway system, which are *always* under construction.

Each night after the amusement park closes the train from underground gold mine ride is used to transport Iowa grown grape extract to Missouri and bring Missouri Corn back to Iowa. The "Iowa Sweet Corn Conspiracy" continued until uncovered by the naive ten (or twelve) year old's simple request for information.

The hypocrisy of the situation caused by the "Iowa Sweet Corn Conspiracy" was that residents of Missouri, Nebraska and Illinois would drive thousands of miles a year to buy "Iowa Sweet Corn" not knowing that it was really "Missouri Corn", thus negating any energy savings created with the Iowa Corn ethanol program.

****

Curse of the Lakota Chief

In 2005 a Lakota Sioux tribal chief from the Rosebud reservation in the Badlands of South Dakota, visited the park and embarked on an experience that the park would never forget, in fact, to this day, the consequences of his visit and his curse recur on a daily basis.

He loved amusement park food and consumed a turkey leg, funnel cake, mini-donuts, kettle corn and whatever else he could lay his hands on. He then proceeded to ride on every ride in the park.

His first adventure was on the Silly Silo, while spinning around stuck to the wall he promptly "forahy", which is the Lakota word for vomited. This started a chain reaction and half the people on the ride joined him in spilling their lunch.

After spending thirty minutes in the men's room cleaning up, he attempted to ride the Side Winder where upon he again got sick while spinning high above the crowd waiting to enter the ride. He barely escaped with his life when three extremely rotund park patrons started chasing him. The only thing that saved him was that he ran fast, as Indians, even seventy-five-year-old Indians, are known to do, to the south sky and escaped to the north side of the park. The three patrons that were chasing him could only run as far as the benches by Puff where they had to sit down and recuperate from their rare burst of physical exercitation.

While on the sky ride a couple of teenage boys in the gondola preceding his were swinging back and forth causing his gondola to also swing, which caused him to get sick yet again. Luckily, he was above a grassy area where there were no park patrons were hit.

He again visited the men's room to clean up and then headed for the Wheel, where the loud screeching noise gave him a headache and the wind made the cars to sway back and forth which caused him once again to get sick.

He then visited the country kitchen for a lunch of fried chicken and beans. After riding on four more rides and getting sick on every one of them, he placed a Lakota curse on the park that declared *"as long as the winds blow and the rivers flow that every day at least ten customer's forahy on park rides."*

To this day the curse has proved to be highly accurate, and the 4A (forahy) was established in tribute to the chief.

****

The Sacred Cahuilla Tribal Stones

This story begins in the summer of 1846, which happened to be the hottest summer anyone could remember. Juan Antonio, Chief of the Cahuilla tribe, conferred with his senior medicine men and they concluded that due to the tribe's dismally low spirits, due to the hot weather, they were in dire need of a spiritual symbol to restore the tribe's spirits. It was decided that they would introduce enchanted sacred rocks which would possess the magical ability to endow prosperity and happiness to whomever possessed them. During the next year the sacred powers of the stones were revered by the tribe and were displayed in a location of prominence in the village. In 1847 they were hidden away in case the tribe lost an upcoming battle against a local enemy as they did not want the sacred stones to fall into the wrong hands. During the Temecula massacre, which was a decisive victory for the tribe, the medicine man that hid the sacred rocks was killed and their hiding place was lost forever, or so they thought.

In the mid 1990's, during the construction of the Jojoba Hills RV Park, the sacred stones were uncovered thus bringing prosperity and happiness to the residents of Jojoba Hills. In 2010, the sacred stones mysteriously appeared on the granite alter at the west end of the Oregon Trail at Jojoba Hills where they remained for the next few years. Every few days they would magically rearrange themselves into a new configuration which allowed the prosperity and pleasure for the Jojoba Hills residents to continue. Then in May of 2012, the stones mysteriously disappeared leaving the residents of Jojoba Hills to
As the bus sped along the jungle road, which snaked its way across the ridge of the mountain, my only thought was that just around the next curve Michel Douglas would emerge from the jungle, draw his shotgun from its holster which was strapped to his back and start blasting the bad guys. As you can tell, my overactive imagination was reliving a scene from the movie "Romancing the Stone". The imagery of traveling on this winding jungle road had dredged up the movie scene from deep within my subconscious memory and played it out vividly in my mind. The scene switched to wildly sliding down a muddy jungle hill and landing headfirst between Sharon Stones legs. I can almost taste the… mud.

What kept this particular movie in my recent sub conscious memory was my visit yesterday to Cartagena, Columbia. In anticipation of the pending visit to the location of some of the scenes from the movie, I had flashbacks of various scenes, but much to my disappointment, in touring the city I saw none of the movie locations.

****

The Briefcase Man

His hair was dark, of medium length and had an unkempt look, much like the rest of his attire. He was wearing a greenish brown herringbone Harris Tweed British country style wool coat the kind that had what looked like a belt sewn onto the mid-section, but it wasn't a belt and it had leather buttons the size of quarters. His trousers were heavy wool which looked like they had lost their crease many months ago. His shoes were brown leather with thick rubber soles because he was on his feet much of the time and he also needed insulation from the cold British weather. He was of medium height, slightly overweight, in his early thirties and he was by himself.

We were in the Anchor Pub on the Cam River in Cambridge, England, and the reason I noticed him was because he was by himself. Most of the patrons were college students and none of them were alone, and all were in deep conversation about politics, string theory and sex.

From a scruffy old brown soft sided leather briefcase, he would extract a sheet of paper, examine it and jot something on it before stuffing it back in the briefcase. This went on for hours with only an occasional break to take a nip from his pint of bitter. While observing him I had tossed down several pints while he was still nursing his original pint.

My first impression was that he was a professor at one of the nearby colleges and he was grading his student's essays on British Literature of the eighteen hundreds or an essay which compares and contrasts British and French Literature of the seventeen hundreds. God, I hated those compare and contracts tests, you have to know what you are talking about, give me a multiple choice any time where at least I have a chance to guess the correct answer.

As I watched him, I noticed he was oblivious to what was going on around him and that he wasn't recording a grade in a grade book for the papers on which he jotted notes. This led me to believe that he was not a professor because no true British professor would waste time by having to go through all the papers a second time to record the grades; they would read the paper, grade it, and enter the grade all in one motion.

****